T0352582

Pære nihte or þæs nihtes? On the interplay of gender shift and declension shift in Old English

Elżbieta Adamczyk, Adam Mickiewicz University

ABSTRACT

A relatively consistent preservation of gender is assumed to have been a salient feature of the process of morphological restructuring of the Old English nominal system: although the paradigmatic (class) affiliation of nouns changed, they essentially tended to preserve their original gender. Accordingly, the manifold *inter*paradigmatic realignments which occurred in the minor (unproductive) inflectional types (mostly) in late Old English entailed primarily parallel shifts in the masculine, neuter and feminine inflection, whereby masculine and neuter stems followed the pattern of the largest masculine and neuter class, the *a*-stems, whereas feminine stems subdued to the impact of the most numerous feminine class – the productive *ō*-stem declension. Such an orderly state of affairs tallies nicely with the (not uncontroversial) principle of gender conservation (Keyser and O'Neil 1985: 104) according to which the analogical transition of nouns from one paradigm to another was accompanied by a consistent preservation of the original gender. While the principle apparently works for some inflectional classes in Old English, such as the *nouns of relationship* which are characterised by a relatively consistent retention of gender (not without exceptions though), it fails to do so for other declensional types, such as the *u*-stems or the *s*-stems. The focus of the present paper is on one of the minor Old English inflectional classes, the root nouns, which will be closely examined with respect to the apparently intricate correlation between gender shift and declensional shift. The investigation seeks to identify and examine the pattern behind the preservation and loss of the original gender, occurring alongside interparadigmatic restructuring. The pattern found in the investigated material proves that gender assignment remained remarkably consistent in this inflectional class, despite the growing analogical pressure from the masculine productive inflection.

1. Introduction

The present paper investigates the fate of grammatical gender in the context of inflectional class realignments which constituted part of a large scale restructuring of the nominal system in Old English. In particular, it discusses the variation in gender displayed by nouns belonging to minor, unproductive inflectional types, occurring alongside the change of declensional affiliation, typical of these nouns, especially in the Late Old English period. The relationship between these two significant features of the Old English nominal system, though fairly straightforward and predictable at first glimpse, turns out to have involved an interplay of a number of interacting factors, contributing eventually to the emergence of the final shape of the English nominal inflection.

The English nominal system, even in its earliest attested stage (i.e., in Old English), was characterised by an increasing lack of stability, which is best manifested in the paradigms of minor declensional types. A range of phonological processes, entailing, among others, the weakening and subsequent loss of vowels in unstressed syllables, incited a reduction of allomorphy within the paradigms and the ensuing lack of case differentiation, leading consequently to a gradual convergence of inflectional classes. The abundantly attested and easily identifiable inter-declensional drift was directed towards the most prevalent noun type, i.e., the *a*-stem declension, which happened to be largely masculine.[1] By the end of the Old English period, the reorganization of the declensional system must have been rather advanced, with the masculine type emerging as the dominant category, attracting nouns affiliated to less stable declensional classes (i.e., the minor, unproductive paradigms). The extent of the resulting erosion of these largely fossilised paradigms seems to vary across individual inflectional classes (cf. the relatively stable class of *nouns of relationship* to a largely disintegrated group of the *u*-stems). The attested migrations of nouns between declensional classes, driven largely by the persistent analogical pressures, were a reflection of a more general restructuring of the morphological system, originating in the Old English period (or even earlier), which embraced a number of developments, the dissolution of grammatical gender being one of the most consequential ones. The process of gradual morphological restructuring of the nominal inflectional system inherited from Proto-Germanic appears to have been a complex development and a number of interacting factors must have been involved therein. Given the prevalence of the masculine declensional type, one could expect that the inter-declensional shift need not have been confined to the extension of masculine inflectional endings as merely signalling the change of declension, but it may well have resulted in an actual change of the original gender of the vacillating nouns. On the contrary, a relatively consistent preservation of gender is assumed to have been a salient feature of the process of morphological restructuring: although the paradigmatic (class) affiliation of nouns changed, they essentially tended to preserve their original gender. Accordingly, the manifold *inter*paradigmatic realignments which occurred in the minor (unproductive) inflectional types (mostly) in late Old English entailed primarily parallel shifts in the masculine, neuter and feminine inflection, whereby masculine and neuter stems followed the pattern of the largest masculine and neuter class, the *a*-stems (< PIE *o*-stems), whereas feminine stems subdued to the impact of the most numerous feminine

---

1   The *a*-stem declension obviously comprised a substantial number of neuter nouns as well. The relative insignificance of the distinction between masculine and neuter in this context was invoked by Lass (1997: 103) who points to the "text-indistinguishability" and the resultant "marginality" of the masculine/neuter opposition in this declensional class, viewing the *a*-stems as "gender-prototypical" (the only difference between the masculine and neuter paradigms being two case endings, i.e., the nominative and accusative pl.).

class – the productive ō-stem declension (< PIE *ā-stems). Such an orderly state of affairs tallies with what can be tentatively called a *principle of gender conservation*, which is, in fact, an observation made by Keyser and O'Neil (1985: 104) to the effect that the analogical transition of nouns from one paradigm to another is accompanied by a consistent preservation of the inherited gender.[2] The "principle" is far from being universal, as the authors admit themselves, adducing Slavic as an example of a language where gender evidently did not prevent nouns from transferring across paradigmatic types, but it seems to be more applicable to the interparadigmatic reshufflings in the early English nominal system (to be verified in the present study).

While the principle apparently works for some inflectional classes in Old English, such as the *nouns of relationship* which seem to be characterised by a relatively consistent retention of gender (due to their semantic integrity), it fails to do so for other declensional classes. The distortion of gender consistency is to be observed, for instance, in the paradigm of *u*-stems, where the originally masculine *winter* 'winter' or *æppel* 'apple' occasionally adopted the inflectional endings of the strong neuter declension (*a*-stems) in the nominative/accusative pl. (*wintru, applu, appla*). By the same token, the analogical pressure of the most expansive masculine *a*-stem inflection is attested in the paradigm of feminine nouns (through the extension of the genitive singular *-es* and the nominative/accusative plural *-as* markers), as in *flōres, flōras* 'floor'. A parallel situation is found in the paradigm of the neuter *s*-stems (*-*es*-/-*os*-stems), where the majority of nouns, alongside the change of paradigmatic membership, lost their original neuter gender exponents, acquiring to a large extent the inflections of the productive masculine *a*-stem paradigm.

The aim of the present paper is to examine the analogical reshufflings in one of the minor inflectional paradigms, the relatively well attested group of root nouns, characterised by a considerable amount of morphophonemic variation in the paradigm, with respect to the apparently intricate correlation between gender shift and declensional shift. The investigation seeks, firstly, to identify and frame the pattern behind the retention and loss of the original gender, occurring alongside inter-declensional transfers in the paradigm of root nouns. Taking a closer look at the quantitative distribution of new (unhistorical) endings in the analysed material, and their incidence in individual substantives will enable to identify the major tendencies in the restructuring process. Secondly, the study will attempt to determine the factors, both class-specific and item-specific when applicable, responsible for the pattern (e.g., the rate or direction of gender/class realignments), emerging from the analysed data. It will be argued that (1) gender assignment remained remarkably consistent in the investigated minor paradigm,

---

2   The same principle seems to be at work in the other Germanic languages. For some details on the Old High German state of affairs, see, for instance, Duke (2005) and Leiss (2000).

despite the growing analogical pressure from the masculine productive inflection, and that (2) the confusion of gender, which is to some extent attested in the examined paradigm, is more likely to be attributed to the pressure from case system of the influential masculine class of *a*-stems rather than viewed as a reflex of a more systematic gender shift.

Prior to any further discussion on the topic, a formal qualification with regard to the terminology used in the present paper seems necessary. The term *gender shift*, known also as *Genuswechsel* in critical literature, will be applied in line with the definition formulated by Jones (1988: 11), where it is viewed as "the reclassification of nominal lexical items under different gender class groupings". Accordingly, it is not to mean a transition from morphological (or grammatical) gender to semantic (or natural) one (which constituted a major and well explored change in the principles of gender assignment in English), but it will refer to the more or less systematic acquisition of a new gender marker by nouns which undergo the process of analogical transference to other declensional types. At the same time, bearing in mind that the essential prerequisite for gender change is an extension of the unhistorical gender forms throughout the paradigm rather than their confinement to one or two categories, one can hardly expect an authentic, systematic shift in gender to occur alongside declensional transfer. The gender change which accompanied morphological class realignments is more likely to have been a relatively unsystematic process, with some haphazard distribution of novel markers, which the present study will attempt to frame. It seems, therefore, more adequate to view such a change of gender in terms of *variation* or *confusion* rather than a genuine *shift*. A final remark concerns the closely intertwined processes of gender and class assignment, which, as suggested by Krygier (2002: 315), should be treated as independent developments operating in a parallel way, with gender being a secondary property, marked externally, i.e., beyond the paradigm. The present study, much as it is focused on the interplay between the two processes, will take this distinction into account, alongside the fact that the Old English gender, as a grammatical category, was not very transparently represented in the inflectional system. The impossibility of any categorical statements about gender and declension affiliation was made explicit by Lass (1997: 108), who alluding to the somewhat disorderly "behaviour of Germanic gender-assignment and noun-declension", concludes that "it's never entirely safe to say that some particular noun N 'was an X-stem of gender G'". The implied gender variation, accordingly, needs to be conceived of not only as a significant feature of the Old English grammatical system, present therein presumably from a very early stage, but also as one which will render any rigid descriptions or classifications problematic.

2. Some remarks on gender in Old English

The gender system of Old English, inherited from Proto-Germanic, is defined as grammatical, with the threefold division into masculine, feminine and neuter. Although such a straightforward definition may imply that the system is rather unproblematic to interpret, on a closer examination it turns out that it was informed by considerable complexity.

The gender of Old English nouns was essentially not assigned on semantic or extralinguistic criteria, such as animacy or sex, but it was based on formal properties. The formal properties did not involve the characteristics of the noun itself, but the agreement patterns between the associated words (i.e., determiners, adjectives, numerals and pronouns), which implies that gender of most nouns was "not predictable from their morphology" (Curzan 2003: 43). More precisely, it was the noun-phrase internal (nouns, relative pronouns, adjectives, demonstrative and possessive pronouns, numerals) and noun-phrase external features (agreement between nouns and verbs, and anaphoric pronouns) that served as potential exponents of the Old English gender (Baron 1971: 120). As the forms of the nominal endings offered limited information about grammatical gender, it was more easily traceable from the forms of the modifiers, i.e., demonstratives, adjectives, numerals and anaphora, rather than inflections. There was neither a *direct* correlation between gender and inflectional class, although both were inherent properties of the noun and an interaction between them did exist. Significantly, gender, signalled by the forms of the attributes (in agreement with the noun), was not indicated by the declensional type to which the noun belonged; quite the contrary, it served as a means (not the primary one though) of ascribing nouns to a particular inflectional class. An exception here is the *s*-stem declension which contained neuter nouns only, the *ō*-stem declension, consisting solely of feminine nouns, and the *nd*-stems which essentially comprised of masculine nouns only (cf. footnote 10). The shape of the nominative sg. could occasionally signal gender, with -*a* marker in the masculine weak nouns, -*u* ending in the feminine nouns, or certain gender-specific derivational suffixes, e.g., feminine -*nes(s)*, masculine -*dōm*, or neuter -*et*, which, however, cannot be viewed as reliable criteria for gender assignment.[3]

The correlation between gender and case has been framed by Kastovsky (2000), who conceives of gender as one of the parameters of Old English noun morphology, which (alongside class) has no overt exponents, and thus needs to "select" exponents of other, overtly marked morphological categories (i.e., case and number), determining thus "the realisation of the categories of case and number within the noun itself, which results in a number of inflectional paradigms..." (Kastovsky 2000: 710). This system of gender marking, though

---

3   Cf. the German system where, with the exception of weak declension, gender emerges as a
     classificatory principle in the nominal system (Duke 2005: 43)

seemingly transparent and potentially efficient, was characterised by a growing lack of consistency, as signalled by Lass (1992: 103): "while the categories of gender, number and case were real enough, it was virtually impossible for any single noun form to be uniquely marked for all three...". The reason for such a state of affairs was an extensive overlap of inflectional markers of different genders and cases, which was to have profound consequences in the subsequent development of the gender system. Undeniably, the gradual loss of gender-specific inflectional forms may be viewed as a critical factor in the reduction of overt gender marking, contributing eventually to a complete obliteration of grammatical gender in English (Kastovsky 2000: 710).[4] When approached from a broader perspective, the unrelating pressure of phonological and morphological (analogical) processes was a major force disturbing the equilibrium of the inherited system, which rendered the existence of a "fully working" gender system and case system eventually impossible (Jones 1988).

A further complication of the initially orderly structured gender system was the presence of nouns of more than one gender (more precisely, displaying the forms of declensional classes of more than one gender), known as *multiple gender nouns* (e.g., *ǣrist* 'resurrection' m.f.n., *lyft* 'air' m.n.f., *flōd* 'flood m.n.*). The attested incongruity of gender forms in one noun has been viewed as a vestige of an earlier state of affairs, implying that all three genders were available at an earlier stage (in Proto-Germanic), but they did not manage to survive in individual Germanic languages (Leiss 2000: 248).[5] Alternatively, the appearance of multiple gender nouns may be viewed as a sign of an imminent demise of the inherited gender system (Sandred 1997: 322), and traced back to two sources: either analogical confusion in particular contexts, or (a vestige of) earlier confusion in the gender system (Mitchell 1986).[6] Finally, Kitson (1990: 185), adducing the

---

4   With reference to the state of affairs after the 10th century, it has been claimed that in the light of this extensive overlap of case and gender markers, "the loss of case and gender formally makes up a single process" (Stenroos 2008).

5   Leiss (2000) makes a recourse to semantic criteria in order to account for the appearance of multiple gender forms, claiming that the semantic ambiguity displayed by these forms can be reduced by assigning them to one of three groupings: count nouns, collective nouns and mass nouns. By way of example, three gender meanings can be identified of Germanic *lyft*, which correspond to the three formal genders: neuter 'air' (mass noun), masculine 'gentle breeze' (count noun) and feminine 'sky' (collective noun) (Leiss 2000: 252).

6   The adequacy of the former source seems to be confirmed by Sandred's (1991) research into irregular inflections in boundary surveys, which leads him to conclude firstly that a "change of inflection is no proof that the appellative itself has undergone a change of gender or has two genders"; and secondly, that a change of inflection is related to the use of the word in a new toponymic context (Sandred 1997: 323, 325). The instances of gender fluctuation, importantly, are attributed to the effects of analogical pressures rather than to change of gender (cf. Coleman (2008) on the change in gender of Old English nouns viewed as "the product of a type of derivational (word-class changing) morphology").

evidence from topographic vocabulary of fully localisable charter boundaries, views gender in Old English as a dialectal variable (1990: 185) and the appearance of multiple gender nouns as a direct consequence thereof.[7] Clearly, such forms testifying to gender fluctuations, alongside the mixed paradigms of nouns which display different genders for the singular and the plural (Lass 1997: 105), are a proof of growing confusion and increasing lack of stability of the Old English gender system.

With regard to the formal status of the Old English gender system, it must be observed that in some cases gender assignment in Old English nouns did involve semantic criteria in accordance with sex affinity, which points to a "partial correspondence between linguistic gender and natural sex alongside gender determined by formal properties" (Curzan 2003: 45). This stays in compliance with a more general statement made by Corbett (1991) who views the coexistence of two gender assignment systems as natural in language, arguing that there are no purely morphological gender systems: once the semantic criteria fail, the morphological properties come into play (Corbett 1991: 34). While in inanimate nouns grammatical gender had little semantic bearing, in animates it tended to coincide with natural gender to some extent, manifested primarily by the anaphoric pronouns (yet, it must be borne in mind that the former group clearly outnumbered the latter).[8] The significance of the extralinguistic motivations, with the pronominal coreference depending on the properties of the referents, can be exemplified, for instance, by the use of feminine anaphoric pronouns to refer to formally neuter *mægden* 'girl', or masculine *wīfmann* 'woman' (Jones 1988: 11; Curzan 2003: 62). On top of it, there seems to be a transparent semantic core for some classes, such as *r*-stems, denoting kinship terms, or *s*-stems, designating mostly names of animals, where gender assignment is based on animacy or sex distinctions. In view of the abovementioned facts, it can be concluded that the semantically and formally based gender assignment rules coincided, resulting in a rather complex and intricate system, foreboding perhaps the later critical development from a morphological assignment system to a semantic one.

Finally, as regards the percentage distribution of Old English nouns with respect to gender, the masculine nouns constituted 45 percent of nouns, the feminine nouns comprised 30 percent and the neuter nouns covered 25 percent of all nouns (Quirk and Wrenn 1957). Given this numerical preponderance as well as the subsequent developments affecting the inherited gender system, the masculine

---

7   An example may be the noun *hyll* 'hill' which is masculine "among the Hwicce and feminine among the West Saxons and Mercian Angles", or *lēah* 'open land', masculine in (Thames Valley) West Saxon and feminine in Anglian and the south eastern area (Kitson 1990: 139, 204).

8   The precedence of semantic criteria is particularly visible in the assignment of gender of personal pronouns in inanimate nouns which, irrespective of their grammatical gender, could take a neuter pronoun.

gender can arguably be viewed as a common gender, "conditioned by the users' preference to attach distinct strong masculine inflectional markers as an alternative set to feminine and neuter nouns" (Wełna 1996: 32).

3. Restructuring of the nominal system: emerging patterns

As the Old English case system was tightly intertwined with the grammatical category of gender, any developments affecting the gender system cannot be analysed without recourse to the changes affecting the inflectional system and vice versa. Accordingly, the analogical reshufflings between declensional classes, brought about by a broadly understood loss of inflection, could be envisaged to have entailed, if not a change of gender, then at least some gender fluctuation. Quite expectedly, the prevalent tendency for nouns to migrate to the masculine *a*-stem class, well attested in the texts from the late Old English period, could be accompanied by a parallel shift to masculine gender. This assumption carries some important, more general implications as to the directionality of any change of gender in a system as the one represented in Old English. Accordingly, with the restructuring of the nominal system, the masculine gender could be seen to represent the dominant category, attracting nouns of obscure gender as well as new loan-words (Lass 1992: 108; Wełna 1980). Such a view was first expounded by Clark (1957: 113), who, drawing on the evidence from the *Peterborough Chronicle* (12th century), postulated that the dissolution of the gender system in Middle English was preceded by *masculinisation*. Not only does this morphological drift towards the masculine *a*-stem declension reflect an extension of the grammatically expressed sex category, but it also gives the masculine gender the status of a default category under this interpretation (Jones 1967). On the other hand, an opposite tendency for nouns to transfer to the neuter category is also identifiable, especially in masculine and feminine inanimate nouns. This alternative process, whereby the neuter nouns tended to fall into definable semantic groups, is known as *neutralisation*, and denotes the dissemination of a feature with no sex-indicating significance (Ross 1936; Steinmetz 2006).[9] These hypotheses postulating divergent directions of gender change, however, irrespective of how plausible and justified they are, stay beyond the direct focus of the present study, which is concerned with formal rather than semantic restructuring of the category of gender.

Traces of unhistorical gender assignment, appearing alongside declensional realignments, are attested in all minor inflectional types in Old English. With reference to Old English *s*-stems, for instance, Schenker (1972: 53) made a claim to the effect that the change of paradigmatic affiliation is often accompanied by

---

9   Curzan (2003: 93) goes as far as to claim that it was the neuter gender that was conceived of as the default category, particularly for inanimate antecedent nouns.

gender reassignment ("mit dem Flexionswechsel geht oft ein Genuswechsel zusammen im Sinn eines Übertritts vom alten Neutrum in das Standardgenus der neuen Flexion"). This statement seems to be relevant to many other declensional classes which testify to the impact of new productive inflection. An exception here is essentially the group of *nd*-stems, comprising of masculine nouns only, where the attachment of feminine or neuter inflectional markers was rather unlikely.[10] Although hardly any vacillation may be expected in the *r*-stems, i.e., *nouns of relationship*, where the semantic factor played a crucial role, some departure from the original state of affairs can be observed. The inflection of neuter *a*-stems turns out to have been almost as attractive to masculine as it was to feminine *r*-stems, with the nominative/accusative pl. *-u* found frequently in *sweostor* 'sister', *dohtor* 'daughter' or *brōþor* 'brother', alongside the masculine genitive sg. *-es* and the nominative/accusative pl. *-as* markers.

Table 1 summarises the major tendencies to be found in individual (minor) declensional classes with respect to gender realignments, presenting a set of nouns which tended to lack stability in terms of gender assignment. The material does not come from an empirical study, but was compiled on the basis of the information found in the standard historical handbooks (Campbell 1959, Brunner 1965) and the *Anglo-Saxon Dictionary* (Bosworth and Toller 1898). It must be emphasised that the data are unlikely to testify to any wholesale gender shift, but they rather bear witness to the presence of more or less regular fluctuation between genders in the paradigm.

DECLENSIONAL CLASS	*EXAMPLES*
i-stems: a. heavy syllable feminine > masculine	*cyst* 'choice', *ēst* 'favour', *hǣst* 'violence', *lyft* 'air', *scyld* 'guilt', *tīd* 'time', *wist* 'sustenance'
b. heavy syllable neuter > feminine (sporadically also masculine)	*wiht* 'creature', *fulwiht* 'baptism', *forwyrd* 'loss', *gebyrd* 'birth', *gecynd* 'race', *gehygd* 'thought', *oferhygd* 'pride', *gemynd* 'memory', *genyht*

---

10   In fact, a few *nd*-stems displayed single feminine forms, manifested in the demonstrative pronoun, e.g., *þēos wealdend*, *þēos fēond*, *to þǣre swelgende*, *sēo timbrend*. In some instances, e.g., in *fēond* or *wealdend*, the feminine forms were used as a direct translation of the Latin expressions, which proves that the feminine construction of these words "was a possibility of the O.E. language" which was never developed (Kärre 1915: 193). It must be noticed, however, that the *nd*-stem nouns can be viewed as having *epicene* gender in that they are masculine in terms of form and inflection, but apply to both feminines and masculines, denoting either sex.

11   A separate category is formed with abstract nouns where the plural *-u* ending is viewed as an indeclinable feminine sg., e.g. *gebyrdu* 'birth', *gecyndu* 'nature', *gewyrhtu* 'work, deed', *oferhygdu* 'arrogance' (Campbell 1959: 244).

	'sufficiency', *geþyld* 'patience', *gewyrht* 'deed' plurals fluctuating between neuter and feminine, without attested singular forms: *giftu* 'marriage', *gehyrstu* 'ornaments', *gedryhtu* 'fortunes'[11]
c. heavy syllable masculine ~ feminine	*sǣ* 'sea'
d. disyllabic i-stems resulting from obscuration of original compounds, vacillating between various genders	*æfest* 'malice' (m.n.), *ǣrist* 'resurrection' (m.f.n.), *weoruld* 'world' (f.m.)
u-stems feminine > masculine masculine > neuter	*flōr* 'floor' winter 'winter' (*wintru*), *æppel* 'apple'
root nouns feminine > masculine	*bōc* 'book', *burh* 'city', *cū* 'cow', *ēa* 'river', *furh* 'fir', *neaht* (nieht) 'night', *sulh* 'plough'
s-stems neuter > masculine	*cealf* 'calf', *ēar* 'ear of grain'
r-stems feminine > masculine	*mōdor* 'mother' *mōdor(es)*
feminine, masculine > neuter	*sweoster* 'sister', *brōþor* 'brother'
nd-stems	no gender vacillation (cf. footnote 10)

As can be observed, in most of the above mentioned substantives the change (or rather variation) in gender assignment takes places clearly in the direction of the masculine type and there are no evident tendencies for masculine nouns to assume any grammatical properties of the feminine. Importantly, although the abovementioned nouns testify to a clear lack of stability in terms of gender assignment, their inflectional variation (mostly the appropriation of masculine inflectional features) is not yet a proof that they did undergo an actual change in gender or displayed two genders. What is more, gender is certainly not to be viewed here as the primary factor which triggered off the unhistorical forms (see the discussion in the forthcoming sections).

There are two other features which cannot go unnoticed when looking at the data and which may furnish some insight into the mechanism of the process of class and gender restructuring. One is related to the fact that gender vacillation, irrespective of the declensional type, is to be observed in nouns of a certain syllable structure, namely heavy syllable stems and disyllabic stems, the latter resulting from the obscuration of original compounds. This very feature accords well with the tendency to be largely observed in the redistribution of nouns over declensional classes, where the heavy syllable stems tend to be more conducive to the encroaching impact of the innovative inflection than their light syllable counterparts (e.g., light vs. heavy syllable *i*-stems (Hogg 1992: 132, 134)). The second characteristic refers to the phonological shape of the nouns in question, where the emergent pattern indicates that the feminine nouns ending in a consonant were more prone to adopt the masculine gender marker than the nouns terminating in a vowel.[12] These very general and tentative observations would need to be verified by a more detailed analysis, taking into account all potential factors which played a part in the gradual restructuring of gender and inflectional class systems. Given the shape of the inflectional class to be analysed in the present study, however, these two correlations cannot be tested (see section 4.1).

With regard to the chronological perspective, the earliest signs of dissolution of the original gender system are to be found in the 10th c., manifested in relatively frequent fluctuation of nouns between genders (Lass 1992: 107). Not surprisingly, the variation may be expected to have been more pervasive in the North where the weakening and decay of inflections occurred earliest.

4. Case study: Root nouns

4.1 Corpus and methodology of the research

As has already been mentioned, the focus of a more detailed investigation is the group of root consonant stems, known also as *mutated plurals*, which at first glance seem to have been characterised by a relatively consistent preservation of gender. The class comprised of nouns of three genders and traces of gender vacillation can be observed in the paradigm of feminine nouns, especially in the subgroup of heavy syllable feminine stems.[13] No traces of feminine inflection are expected to be found in the masculine paradigm. They seem highly unlikely bearing in mind the fact that the declension shift in the minor paradigms was determined by the preponderance of the masculine type.

The feminine subgroup of the root noun declension included the following nouns: *āc* 'oak', *bōc* 'book', *brōc* 'trousers', *burg* 'borough', *cū* 'cow', **dung* 'prison', *ēa* 'river', *furh* 'furrow, ditch', *gāt* 'goat', *gōs* 'goose', *grūt* 'groats',

---

12 This seems to comply with a theory postulated by Jones (1967: 290) who emphasises the significance of the structure of the nouns in *Genuswechsel*, drawing attention to the fact that the nominal heads ending in a vowel were historically usually classified as feminine, and, therefore, analogical pressure may have worked towards rendering nouns of such a structure feminine; whereas nominal heads terminating in a consonant, which were more commonly classified as masculine, tended to change to masculine gender.

13 As regards the neuter inflection which could potentially display masculine features, not much can be deduced from the available material; in fact, the neuter inflection, but for one noun (*scrūd* 'cloth(es)'), is non-existent. The lone representative patterns as a regular member of the strong neuter declension, with the endingless nominative/accusative pl.

hnitu 'nit', *hnutu* 'nut', *lūs* 'louse', *meolc* 'milk', *mūs* 'mouse', *neaht* (*niht*) 'night', *studu* (*stuðu*) 'pillar', *sulh* 'plough', *turf* 'turf', *þrūh* 'trough', *wlōh* 'fringe'. The scope of the quantitative analysis includes the evidence provided by the early English material as edited in the *Dictionary of Old English* electronic corpus (Healey 2004). The focus of the investigation was on the quantitative relation between the incidence of the inherited inflectional endings and the innovative *a*-stem and *ō*-stem markers in the paradigm and, within the latter group, on the distribution of the masculine and feminine inflectional exponents in the paradigm, both in the head noun and in the adnominal phrase. In order to frame the changes in gender assignment in the context of declensional realignments, the examination took into account the congruential gender criteria, to use the terminology of Jones (1967: 19), namely, the relationship between the pre- and post-head modifiers, and the head word of the nominal group.

When it comes to investigating gender variation from the perspective adopted in the present study, formal rather than semantic factors seem to be of primary importance. The grammatical categories where gender vacillation, occurring alongside the declensional class change, can be identified are the genitive and dative sg. Not all grammatical categories can be equally informative with respect to gender, however. Accordingly, the nominative sg. (of heavy syllable stems) can provide little information about gender in the context of declension class shift, as its shape cannot be influenced by the innovative inflection in any way. Much as the accusative sg. may testify to the presence of novel inflection, it does not (or is very unlikely to) offer any insight into the accompanying gender vacillation, as the novel forms could be feminine only.[14] Likewise, no forms can be unambiguously recognised with respect to gender in the plural, therefore, the category of the plural was not taken into account in the quantitative investigation. Finally, the adoption of weak inflectional endings cannot provide reliable information about gender realignments, as the distribution of the *-an* and *-ena* markers was very similar for the three gender classes. Finally, to some extent, an attempt at accounting for unhistorical gender agreement necessitates individual, lexeme-specific approach as various idiosyncratic factors may have been at work in the restructuring process, rendering a given account be relevant to some lexical items, not to others.

---

14   Potentially, the new masculine gender could be reflected in the form of the accusative sg. when under the influence of the *n*-stem inflection (with the *-an* marker, e.g., **þone nihtan*); however, no such instances were found in the investigated material.

4.2 Declensional realignments in the Old English root nouns

Although the analogical developments affected the paradigm of both masculine and feminine nouns, for reasons mentioned above, the present investigation is confined to the paradigm of the latter subgroup. The potential traits of interparadigmatic realignments to be found in the feminine paradigm entail primarily the features extended from the productive feminine inflection of *ō*-stems as well as from the most expansive inflection of masculine *a*-stems. Accordingly, the shape of the feminine paradigm may potentially have been distorted by the appearance of the following features:

feminine features	*masculine features*
– the original endingless genitive sg. of long syllable stems replaced by -*e*	– the original endingless genitive sg. of long syllable stems replaced by -*es*
– the dative sg. -*e* in place of the original endingless dative form (long syllable stems)	– the dative sg. -*e* in place of the original endingless dative form (long syllable stems)
– the accusative sg. -*e* marker in place of the endingless form (long syllable stems)	– the nominative/accusative pl. -*as* ending in place of the endingless umlauted form (long syllable stems)
– the nominative/accusative pl. -*a*/-*e* ending in place of the endingless umlauted form (long syllable stems)	
– the nominative sg. -*u* ending in place of etymological zero ending (short syllable stems)	
– weak -*an* ending in all cases in the singular (except the nominative) and in the nominative/accusative pl.	
– weak -*ena* ending in the genitive pl.	

All of these potential innovative features are summarised in Table 2 which presents the two competing paradigms for the OE *burg/h* 'town', adduced here as a very well attested representative of the whole subclass of long-syllable feminine stems.

Table 2. The competing paradigms of the Old English feminine root nouns (long syllable stems)

	archaic		*innovative*	
	singular	*plural*	*singular*	*plural*
nominative	burh/g	byrh/g	burh/g	burge, **-as**, **-a(n)**
genitive	byrg	burga	burge, **-es**, **-an**	burga, **-ena**
dative	byrg,byrig	burgum	burge, **-an**	burgum
accusative	burh/g	byrh/g	burge, **-an**	burge, **-as**, **-a(n)**

The above-presented forms testify to the presence of two opposing forces in the paradigm of root nouns, which surely played a part in the gradual reshaping of the inherited paradigm. On the one hand, the allomorphic variation present in the paradigm, with mutated vowels in the genitive and dative sg. and the nominative/accusative pl., constituted a distinctive feature which worked most likely towards the retention of the inherited inflection. Clearly, with such a distinctive shape of the paradigm, the root nouns "had the potential to retain formal case-marking" (Hogg 1997: 106). On the other hand, the syncretism of the nominative and accusative in the singular and the plural was a competitive feature which worked to the detriment of the integrity of the paradigm, facilitating the activity of analogical processes, both external and internal. What is more, as a result of analogical reshaping within the paradigm, the syncretised forms of the genitive and dative sg., with unmutated vowel, began to emerge, depriving the paradigm of the original morphophonological diversity. In a broader context, this growing syncretism of nominal categories (to be observed not only in the paradigm of root nouns, but across all declensional classes) was a major factor which rendered the nouns vulnerable to analogical pressures, effecting the change of declensional affiliation as well as the closely related variation in gender.

4.3 Results of the investigation and discussion

Prior to presenting the results of the quantitative investigation, it must be observed that the small group of short syllable stems was analysed separately; the impact of innovative inflection in these three, scantily attested nouns (*hnitu, hnutu* and *studu*) can potentially be detected in the nominative sg., where synchronic alternation between the archaic endingless form and the arguably novel *u*-ending, extended from the feminine *ō*-stem paradigm, is attested (e.g., *stud ~ studu*). Apart from this direction of change, analogical sway of the weak inflection is also occasionally found in the genitive pl. (e.g., *hnutena*). Significantly, no impact of the masculine inflectional pattern could be identified in these stems, and, consequently, none of these forms could impart any reliable information about gender variation. Accordingly, the systematic quantitative investigation concentrated exclusively on the paradigm of long syllable feminine stems, and the findings presented below are confined to this relatively well attested subgroup of root nouns.

Table 3 below depicts the distribution of archaic and innovative inflection, where the innovative features comprise traces of the *a*-stem, *ō*-stem and *n*-stem declension. The findings come from a separate study conducted systematically on the complete corpus of Old English texts for the entire class of root nouns (Adamczyk, in prep.). Their inclusion here is to serve as a background for further discussion and a point of reference for the analysis proper in the sense that they offer insight into the overall condition of the root noun paradigm with respect to restructuring, including the information about the distribution of archaic and innovative features in the plural which, for reasons mentioned above, will not be the subject of the current analysis. Only the cases in which synchronic alternation between the inherited and novel inflection was attested are presented.

Table 3. Distribution of archaic and innovative inflection in the feminine root noun paradigm irrespective of gender markers (long syllable stems)

	inherited inflection	innovative inflection
genitive sg.	(162) 21.2%	(602) 78.8%
dative sg.	(1672) 77.1%	(496) 22.9%
accusative sg.	(1559) 97%	(49) 3%
nominative pl.	(243) 91.8%	(21) 8.2%
accusative pl.	(512) 84.8%	(92) 15.2%
total	**76.7%**	**23.3%**

The data clearly indicate that the root noun paradigm remains relatively impervious to analogical readjustments on the pattern of the productive inflection. The genitive sg. is the only case in the paradigm of *mutated plurals* which was seriously affected by the new inflection, which is indicative, however, of the presence of declensional shift rather than gender vacillation (cf. Table 4 below).

Although the detailed discussion of the reasons for the attested inflectional archaism of this class of nouns remains essentially beyond the scope of the present study, two critical factors need to be mentioned in this context. One has to do with the morphophonological shape of the root nouns, i.e., the presence of mutated vowel both in the singular and the plural, which, as was envisaged, acted as a force precluding a more radical disintegration of the original paradigm. The other factor responsible for the relative conservatism of this declensional type is the frequency of occurrence of its members, which may have had a conserving effect, in compliance with the principle holding that "high frequency units are resistant to reformation on the basis of productive patterns" (Bybee 1985, 1995; Bybee and Hopper 2001) (e.g., *burh, bōc, neaht*). The attested archaism evinced by the root noun paradigm is reminiscent of the situation found in the small group of conservative Old English *r*-stems, which retained the inherited inflection in roughly 60 percent (60.3%) of forms (Adamczyk 2009). Here also the remarkable resistance to the impact of productive inflection can be attributed to the frequency factor and the fact that the group, though small, contained nouns characterised by very high frequency of occurrence (in texts, but possibly also in use) (*mother, father, sister, brother*, etc.).

Table 4 presents the findings from the quantitative investigation into gender confusion occurring alongside inter-declensional transfers in the class of root nouns with respect to individual cases, whereas Table 5 provides the overall results for the singular, irrespective of case distinctions. The tables offer two sets of results: one for the overall class, and the other excluding the attestation for *neaht*. Such an approach was considered necessary for two reasons, one of them being the relatively high frequency of *neaht*, much higher than the frequency of other nouns in the investigated class; whereas the other reason had to do with the fact that the attestation for the genitive sg., where *neaht* displays a clear pattern motivated by semantic criteria (see the discussion below), would have skewed the final findings. While the feminine and masculine inflection, with gender distinctive markers on the head noun, could be easily identified in the genitive sg., no such gender specific exponents exist for the dative sg. (where *-e* serves as the case marker for both masculine and feminine nouns) and, consequently, the figure for the dative sg. does not embrace gender distinction.

Table 4. Distribution of archaic and innovative inflection with respect to gender for individual cases in the singular

	inherited inflection	new inflection		new gender marker
		feminine	*masculine*	*(masculine)*
genitive sg.	(161) 21%	(340) 56%	(267) 44%	(10) 1.6%
(without *neaht*)	(154) 37.9%	(228) 90.5%	(24) 9.5%	
		masculine/feminine		
dative sg.	(1614) 76.5%	(496) 23.5%		(2) 0.4%
(without *neaht*)	(1386) 93%	(104) 7%		
accusative sg.	(1542) 96.90%	(49) 3.1%		–
(without *neaht*)	(1084) 99.5%	(5) 0.5%		

Table 5. Overall distribution of archaic and innovative inflection with respect to gender

	inherited inflection	new inflection	new gender marker
singular	(3317) **74.2%**	(1152) **25.8%**	(12) **1.03%**
(without neaht)	(2624) **87.9%**	(361) **12.1%**	

As becomes evident, traces of gender fluctuation (attested beyond the head noun) in the class of root nouns are very sporadic and appear primarily in the genitive sg., where they constitute 1.6 percent of the all the innovative inflection in the paradigm. Along with the forms found in the dative sg., they make up roughly 1 per cent of all innovative forms. Although the accusative sg. could potentially testify to gender variation, no traces of masculine inflection were identified in the analysed material.[15]

---

15   In the case of texts which are translations from Latin (involving a literal Latin gloss), some

The exclusion of the data for *neaht* from the total count turns out to be very informative with respect to the presence of new inflection in the paradigm. The discrepancy is significant especially for the genitive and dative sg., where the incidence of innovation reaches 79 percent and 23.5 percent, respectively, when *neaht* is included, relative to respective 62.1 percent and 7 percent, when it is discarded from the analysis. Likewise, the high percentage of new masculine features found in the genitive sg. (head noun), amounting to 44 percent, is attributable to the form *neahtes* (*nihtes*), frequently attested in the adverbial phrase with *dæg*, and decreases significantly to 9.5 per cent when the data for *neaht* is detracted.

When taking a closer look at the distribution of archaic and innovative inflection in individual root nouns, a number of observations are in order. Hardly any traces of novel inflection were found in the paradigms of *brōc* '(the) breech'[16], **dung* 'prison' (not found in the investigated corpus at all, cf. Bosworth and Toller (1898), s.v. *dung*), *grūt* 'groats', *lūs* 'louse', *turf* 'turf', *wlōh* 'fringe'.[17] In fact, no conclusive statements about gender variation in these nouns can be arrived at, as they are attested in contexts which reveal no information about the attributive or anaphoric usage.[18] As regards the remaining nouns from this declension, the following patterns could be identified for individual items in the course of the investigation:

(a) *ǣc*: two innovative forms found in the genitive and dative sg. (*ǣce*), gender consistently preserved;

(b) *bōc*: The innovative forms are very rare given the overall frequency of attestation of the noun and appear primarily in the genitive sg., testifying to the impact of both feminine and masculine inflection, and sporadically

---

impact of the Latin gender on the gender of Old English nouns cannot be excluded. Although this aspect was not subject to any special scrutiny in the present investigation, no significant correlations have been detected which could influence the general pattern. Such external influence is certainly of more importance in the subsequent period, i.e., early Middle English. There, as claimed by Wełna (1980), transfers of nouns from one gender to another are to a greater extent to be attributed to the contact with French and Latin (Wełna 1980: 400; cf. Millar 2002: 302-303; Stenroos 2008: 466).

16   One weak form was identified in the investigated material, namely the genitive sg. *brēcena*, attested in the following context: *Brecena* tancen is þæt þu strice mid þinum twam handum up on þin þeah (Notes 2).

17   A single innovative form is attested in the genitive pl. (*wgloana*), formed on the pattern of the weak productive inflection. An unambiguous interpretation of the gender of this noun is actually problematic, but the noun has been traditionally classified as feminine (Bosworth and Toller (1898); Hall (1960)). The new analogical form does not provide any insight in this respect either.

18   Notice that the discrepancy in the results for the attestation of archaic features in the dative and accusative sg. between Tables 3 and 4 results precisely from the fact that the abovementioned nouns were not included in the analysis.

in the dative sg. (*bōce* 4x) and the accusative pl. (*bōce* 2x). Infrequent traces of weak inflection are attested, e.g., in the genitive sg. (*bōcan*) and the genitive pl. (*bōcana, bōcenæ*). Apart from the presence of masculine inflection, traces of neuter forms are also to be found, for instance, in the accusative sg., as illustrated by the following sentence:

(1)   *et ut reuoluit librum inuenit loco ubi scribtum erat* & þætte ł miððy untynde þæt **boc** gemitte to stoue ðer awritten wæs. (LkGl (Li))[19]

The not infrequently attested unmutated forms of the dative sg. (*bōc*) are not treated as innovative in the present investigation. They certainly can be viewed as an indication of restructuring of the inflectional system, but are to be attributed to internal pressures of analogy, i.e., the intraparadigmatic developments, occurring within the paradigm rather than, more pertinent to the present study, interparadigmatic ones, taking place across the inflectional paradigms.[20]

(c) *burh* (*burg*): The sporadically appearing *-as* plural forms of *burh* are attested in the Anglian texts, in particular in the Northumbrian glosses. The masculine *-es* marker appears only when *burg* is a part of a proper name (e.g., *Sunnanburges, Kyneburges*); otherwise the noun attaches only feminine inflectional endings in the paradigm of the singular. The high incidence of the form *byrig* (33.4%) is responsible for a relatively high percentage of archaic inflection in the dative sg. (see Table 4).

(d) *cū*: There are some single instances of the spread of the masculine genitive *-es* marker; these three identified occurences (*cūs, cuus*) are attested in Late West-Saxon texts dated to the 11th c. At the same time, forms such as *cūe* in the genitive sg. or *cȳe* in the accusative pl., found already in the *Vespasian Psalter* (mid-9th c.), testify to a sporadic analogical spread of the strong feminine inflection in the paradigm. The

---

19   The use of the abbreviations in the present section follows the practice of Cameron (1973), who provides a complete list of texts cited in the *Dictionary of Old English* corpus, with short titles and detailed bibliographic information. For an updated list of texts see also the homepage of the *Dictionary of Old English* project at: http://www.doe.utoronto.ca /st/index.html.

20   The noun tended to be unstable with respect to gender, showing different affiliation in individual Germanic languages. Accordingly, in Old Frisian and Old Saxon the noun *bôk* vacillates between neuter and feminine, whereas in Old High German *buoh* is attested as neuter and occasionally declines as feminine and masculine. It is assumed that originally the noun had a feminine gender and derived from PGmc.*bôks and the neuter gender was initially introduced into the plural probably by analogy to monosyllabic neuter nouns and subsequently extended to the singular (cf. OHG light masculine *ja*-stems which tended to shift to neuter declension: *heri* 'army', *wekki* 'wedge', *meri* 'lake') (Bammesberger 1990: 197-8; Lahiri and Dresher1983: 143, 160).

new inflectional marker is found in the head noun in all instances and there are no accompanying features in the adnominal phrase, which could provide cues about gender. The pressure of the weak inflection is remarkable in the genitive pl., where forms such as *kuna* and *kyna* are prevailing (the umlauted forms being actually more frequent), which do not, however, offer any reliable information about gender.[21]

(e) *ēa*: The paradigm is abundant in innovative features, attested in the genitive, dative and accusative sg. as well as in the plural, where alongside innovative inflection extended from the feminine *ō*-stems (*ēae* 2x), the weak inflectional marker is attested (*ēan*) in late West-Saxon material; the new masculine inflectional marker appears in the genitive sg. (*ēas* 7x), but no traces of masculine gender are found beyond the head noun.

(f) *furh*: the novel inflection attested in the genitive sg. (*furghs*, *fures*), with the feminine gender preserved consistently on the demonstrative pronoun; the weak inflectional marker found also in the genitive pl. (*furan* 3x);

(g) *gāt*: The novel inflectional forms appear only in the genitive sg. (*-e*) and testify to the impact of feminine inflection only; two attested instances can be unambiguously identified as feminine thanks to the presence of contextual cues (demonstrative pronouns).

(h) *gōs*: innovative (feminine) features found in the genitive sg. only (*gōse*); no impact of the masculine inflection detected in the paradigm;

(i) *meolc*: innovative forms attested in the genitive and dative sg. (*meolce*, *meoluce*), with no clear indication of gender;

(j) *mūs:* innovative feminine forms attested in the genitive sg. ((*-*)*muse* 2x), and sporadic traces of weak inflection found in the accusative pl. (attested once as *musen* in charters (Ch 959));

(k) *sulh*: The novel masculine forms are found in the genitive sg. (*sules* 2x) and occur alongside the innovative feminine *-e* marker (*sule reost* vs. *sules reost*). The impact of weak productive inflection is also found in the genitive sg. (*sylan* 1x, *sylan scear* and *sulan* 3x), however, no information about gender is retrievable from the context.

(l) *prūh*: two innovative forms of the dative sg. attested (*prūge*), one of them testifying to gender variation (in the demonstrative pronoun); some traces of innovative inflection found in the nominative and accusative pl. (3x);

---

21 Given that the weak inflectional pattern became prevalent in the paradigm of *cū* in the subsequent Middle English stage (*kyne*, *kyen*, *kyn*), an evident dearth of weak forms in the nominative and accusative pl. in the Old English material seems unexpected. Notice the consistent preservation of the mutated root vowel alongside the appropriation of the weak inflectional endings, which must have been a factor responsible for retention of such relic forms as *kine*.

The limited number of novel forms found in the examined material can be attributed to the dynamics of the restructuring of this declensional type, which turned out to have been rather archaic with respect to the reorganisation of the case system. What can be easily observed is a relatively low proportion of forms in which gender is explicitly marked; when such explicit marking occurs, gender is most often reflected in the category of the demonstrative pronoun, or, much less commonly, in the adjective. Although anaphoric reference was also taken into consideration in the course of the investigation, no instances of gendered anaphoric usage were found in the analysed material.[22]

It may be concluded that the attested pattern of preservation of the etymological gender in the investigated material testifies to the fact that gender system did not suffer any major distortion alongside the declensional shift in the class of root nouns. The attested occasional variation is too scant to allow identification of any discernible pattern which would reflect a systematic change in gender. At the same time, the available data admits of framing the mechanism of gender variation in the context of declensional transfers, provided that also the gender-distinctive inflectional markers can serve as a tentative source of information about gender fluctuation. Accordingly, the variation found in the investigated material allows identifying three distinct developments, entailing: (1) the extension of the new masculine forms to the head noun, signalling, primarily and most likely, no more than the impact of a new inflectional pattern (class), not necessarily of a new gender, (2) the extension of the new masculine forms to the head noun, and the accompanying preservation of the inherited gender on the pre- or post-modifier, and (3) the extension of the new inflection to the head noun *and* to the pre- or post-modifier, which might signal the change in gender, most likely sporadic rather than systematic. The following section serves to illustrate the above-discussed developments:

(i) new functional marker – gender not marked overtly

The spread of a new functional marker, extended from the masculine *a*-stem inflection, is well substantiated by the forms of the genitive sg. and nominative/ accusative pl., as illustrated by sentences (2)-(5) and (6)-(7), respectively. Much as such instances can disclose about interparadigmatic realignments, they are hardly informative about the change in gender assignment. Although the variation in the shape of the head noun may potentially lead in the end to a change in gender assignment, such a course of events is not automatically warranted.

---

22 Gender is believed to have been retained longer in the anaphoric pronouns than in the noun phrase (Stenroos 2008: 459). Any vacillation between genders is thus more likely to be first reflected noun-phrase internally, e.g., in the determiner system.

(2)   oxan tægl bið scillinga weorð, **cus** bið fifa; oxan eage bið V pæninga weorð, **cus** bið scilling weorþ. (LawInc)

(3)   Be **cuus** horne. (LawIneRb)[23]

(4)   Dentalia **sules** reost (ClGl 1)

(5)   Næs hweðre nænig man þe þær æfre **nihtes** tidum dorste on þære ciricean cuman (LS 25)

(6)   Þas **bocas** haueð Salomon preost, þæt is þe codspel traht & þe martyrliua & þe æglisce saltere & þe cranc & ðe tropere ... (Rec 5.5)

(7)   (Et circumibat iesus ciuitates omnes et castella) & ymbeade ðe hælend ceastræ vel **burgas** alle (MtGl (Li))

(8)   (et huic ait et tu esto supra quinque ciuitates) & ðissum cuoeð & ðu wæs ofer fif **burgas** (LkGl (Li))

The dissemination of the strong feminine marker -*e*, in compliance with the assumption that class realignment observes gender distinctions (when considered from inflectional point of view only), can be found, for instance, in the genitive sg. (examples 9-10) and the accusative pl. (example 11):

(9)   To ælcum dolge sealf, gesomna **cue** mesa, cu migoþa, gewyrce to flynan þa swa mon sapan wyrcð micelne citel fulne... (Lch II (1))

(10)   Wiþ ban ece, tuningwyrt, beolone, wealwyrt, ealde grut & eced, heorotes smera oþþe **gate** oþþe **gose**, meng tosomne, lege þonne on. (Lch II (1))

(11)   ðu ðreades wuda gemot fearra betwih **cye** folca ðæt ne sien utatyned ðas ða gecunnade werun seolfre (Increpa feras siluarum concilium taurorum inter uaccas populorum ut non excludantur...) (PsGlA (Kuhn))[24]

The new inflectional marker in the dative sg. (-*e*) cannot be unambiguously identified as masculine or feminine unless gender is signalled by some contextual cues, i.e., forms other than the head noun. Consequently, these novel dative sg. forms testify primarily to the presence of new inflection, offering no information whatsoever about gender, e.g.,

(12)   his heafod mon lædde to Lindesfearena **eae**, & þær in cirican bebyrgde; (Bede 3)

(13)   Maria seo Magdalenissce sohten urne drihten mid smerigeles inne his **þruge**, þa þa he bebyriged wæs. (HomU56)

---

23   An alternative interpretation of *cus*, as attested in the phrase *cus horn*, has been offered by Griepentrog (1994: 239), who views it as a part of a compound formation, in which -*s* serves as a *Fugenkonsonant*. This interpretation may be supported by the fact that a compound *cuhorne* exists in parallel manuscripts.

24   See Griepentrog (1994: 239) for the possibility of the influence of the *i*-stem declension here.

(ii) new functional marker – preserved gender

The new functional marker alongside which the original gender can be unambiguously identified is attested in the genitive sg., testifying to the impact of both masculine (examples 14-19) and feminine inflection (examples 20-24), as well as in the dative sg. (examples 25-27). The attestation for the genitive sg., with the masculine *-es* marker extended from the productive *a*-stem inflection, is a clear instance of lack etymological congruence between the inflectional form and gender.

(14) on heæfde **þere boces** awriten is be me tunc (dixi ecce venio in capite libri scriptum est de me) (PsGlE)

(15) andlang weges up on Coccan burh of **þære burhges** gete on Hengestes heafod. (Ch 141)

(16) het atimbran þa burg on suþ healfe **þære eas** ær he þonan fore: (ChronA (Plummer))

(17) for þæm ðæt land wæs eall gebun on oþre healfe **þære eas**. (Or1)

(18) þanne an lang **þere fures** one dat dich & þanen to tatanbeorge. (Ch 429)

(19) Endlang **þer furghs** to þan bourne þanen endlang borne as (Ch 541)

(20) nim þonne apuldorrinde & æscrinde, slahþornrinde & wirrinde & elmrinde & holenrinde & wiþigrinde & **geongre ace**, sealhrinde do þa ealle on micelne citel... (Lch II (1))

(21) Her onginnað þa capitulas **þære** forman **boce** (GDHead 1 (H))

(22) ...wege hi and sete þine swyþran ofer þine wynstran earm be **þære boce** læncge. (Notes 2)

(23) Wið nædran slite, sceaf gate horn on þry scenceas & **þare ylcan gate** meolc wið wine gemencgede on þry siþas drince. (Med 1.1)

(24) Þisse adle eac wiþstandeþ **tosnidenre hreaþemuse** blod gesmiten on þæs seocan mannes wambe. (LchII (2))

(25) Eac we onfundun þæt sume men of **ðære meolce** þysse ylcan wyrte heora eagan smyredon & him þy sel wæs (Lch I (Herb))

(26) And of **þære æce** on þæne hearapod. (Ch 651)

(27) Affrica onginð, swa we ær cwædon, eastan westwerd fram Egyptum æt **þære ee** þe man Nilus hæt. (Or1)

(iii) new functional marker – new gender marker

The following set of examples presents a handful of novel forms which unambiguously testify to gender fluctuation. The extension of the new gender marker is confined to the genitive (sentences 28-34) and dative sg. (sentences 35-36).

(28) & cwæð þæt þær wæs færlice gecuman word fram þan casere þæt heo
sceolden beon ofslagene **þæs** ilcan **nlhtes** (LS 29 (Nicholas))

(29) giinlihta we bid' driht' ðiostro vsra & **alles næhtes** giseto ðv eft f'drif
mildelice. (DurRitGl 1)

(30) He com to him **anes nihtes** on swefne swyðe brihte scinende (LS 28 (Neot))

(31) & ilca gear **anes nihtes** feorme ouðer XXX scyllinge penega, swa eac þet
eafter his dæi scolde seo land ongean into þa mynstre. (ChronE (Irvine))

(32) het him þæt he hæfde geare þa þri cnihtes onsundrig fram oðrum mannum
þæt he hio **þæs oðres nihtes** dearnelice ofslean mihte. (LS 29 (Nicholas))

(33) ...ve gibiddað þætte ðerh ðas of' **tocymendes næhtes** heolstrvng ðin vsig
gescilda ðiv sviðra þætte on lehtes armorgenlic allo arise ve gefeande.
(DurRitGl 2)

(34) Nim þonne þæt sæd, sete on **þæs sules** bodig, cweð þonne. (MCharm 1)

(35) þa wearð se erchebisceop dæd of **þæm** godan **burge** þe is gehaten Mirrea
(LS 29 (Nicholas))

(36) Soð hit is þæt ic hine abæd and on clænen syndonissce hræigle befeold and
hine on **minen þruge** geleigde. (Nic (C))

The data indicate clearly that the paradigm stayed under the influence of both
feminine and masculine productive inflection, and, accordingly, alongside the
expected mutated vowels in cases such as the dative sg. or the nominative/
accusative pl., the new feminine and masculine forms are attested. The
examination of the congruential gender criteria in the investigated material reveals
that the inherited gender system, while disturbed by interparadigmatic
realignments, was preserved unaffected by any radical developments. In fact, very
few instances of forms testifying to new gender agreement patterns were found in
the investigated material. The presence of the masculine inflection appears to have
been sporadic and irregular, and in view of the limited number of instances where
gender changes alongside the extension of a new inflectional marker, the attested
variation can hardly be indicative of gender reassignment in this group of nouns.
None of the investigated substantives testifies to a radical departure from their
inherited gender and, significantly, none, but for *bōc* (see example 1 and footnote
20), shows gender variation in the nominative sg., which could otherwise be
indicative of some major development going on in gender assignment. If any
gender realignment is attested, it affects only the genitive and dative sg., as
illustrated by sentences (28) – (36).

    Given the nature of analogical change, its sporadicity and the fact that it often
involves lexically particular developments, an individual approach to particular
members of the class is necessary in order to account for the (ir)regularity within
the paradigm. Such an approach seems to be particularly relevant to the Old
English *neaht/niht* 'night', where the extension of masculine inflection seems to
have been contextually conditioned. On the one hand, being a frequently attested

word (which implies high frequency of use), the noun can be expected to have retained the inherited pattern of inflection, evincing the etymological class and gender affiliation. On the other, it turns out that factors other than morphological have played a role in the shape of the paradigm of *neaht*. Accordingly, the proximity of the masculine *a*-stem *dæg* 'day', with the genitive sg. *-es* marker and the semantic connection between the two nouns, largely influenced the formal profile of the paradigm of *neaht*. Although most of the forms attaching the masculine *-es* marker are attested in adverbial phrases with *dæg* 'day', exemplified by sentences (37) - (40), there are a number of instances where *neaht* is found in a more independent context, without the accompanying *dæg*, as illustrated by examples (28) - (33) above.

(37) þa namen hi þa men þe hi wenden ðæt ani god hefden. bathe be **nihtes** & be **dæies**. (ChronE (Plummer))

(38) For ðon **deges** & **naehtes** gehefegad is ofer me hond ðin gecerred ic eam in ermðu ðonne bið gebrocen ðorn (Quoniam die ac nocte grauata est super me manus tua, conuersus sum in erumna dum confringitur spina) (PsGlA)

(39) ond he ma gewunade in his smiðþan **dæges** & **nihtæs** sittan (Bede 5)

(40) Witodlice þære eadigan femnan Eufrosinan ben wæs to Gode **dæges** and **nihtes**, þæt heo næfre on hire life gecyðed wære. (LS 7 (Euphr))

A similar external motivation for the attested pattern of inflection can be identified for the nouns *burg* and *ēa*, which being terrestrial landmarks (alongside nouns such as *eorðe* 'earth', *woruld* 'world'), are considered to be *resilient* nouns by virtue of their resistance to the effects of distance, following grammatical gender independently of how far the anaphoric pronoun appears from the antecedent noun (Curzan 2003: 100).[25] The attestation of these nouns in the context relevant for the present study, i.e., alongside declensional realignments, does not provide any conclusive evidence to corroborate this assumption, nevertheless, when considered from purely inflectional perspective, both *burg* and *ēa* indeed turn out to be resistant to external influence, adopting the novel inflection in 9.6 and 6.4 percent of forms, respectively.

4. Concluding remarks

The aim of the paper was to frame the correlation between change in gender and change in the inflection class membership in the paradigms which, due to their lack of productivity, were susceptible to a large scale restructuring. The study sought to investigate to what extent the root nouns show variation in grammatical

---

25 Nouns denoting celestial bodies (e.g., *sunne* 'sun', *mona* 'moon') and temporal phenomena (e.g., *dæg* 'day'), as well as *cirice* 'church' follow the same principle (Curzan 2003: 100).

gendei agrccment, with a view to measuring the extent to which the historical gender was lost or preserved alongside the transfer of nouns to the productive declensional classes (*a*- and *ō*-stems).

While the material does show some variation in the use of gendered forms, the scantily attested irregularity is far from reflecting a systematic gender change. What can be stated about the attested interparadigmatic realignments, in general, is that some evident masculinisation tendencies are displayed by nominal forms, manifested in their adoption of patterns and forms associated with the strong masculine category (such as the extension of the *-es* and *-as* endings). However, the attested variation reflects primarily the reorganisation of the formal system (case system), with the growing syncretism of nominal categories, and the competition between declensional types rather than any major reorganisation taking place within the category of gender. Significantly, it must be observed that the amount of the novel inflection in the paradigm of root nouns is largely limited and the class, albeit fossilised and entirely unproductive, is far from losing its identity as an independent declensional type.

The attested developments can be summarised in the following way: in most investigated nouns, what we deal with is the prevalence of the case exponent rather than gender marker. Accordingly, the *-es* or the plural *-as* markers, with their considerable analogical force, are not primarily indicators of gender in the investigated nouns, but merely case markers, emerging under the growing pressure of the most productive inflectional type, i.e., the masculine *a*-stems. This is confirmed by the examination of the use of the attributives, which reveals that in hardly any of the investigated nouns is the new gender manifested by the application, for instance, of a new demonstrative pronoun; instead, the variation is predominantly expressed by the extension of the masculine *a*-stem markers to the head nouns themselves. Furthermore, given that the diffusion of the unhistorical gender forms *throughout* the paradigm is a prerequisite for gender change (Jones 1967: 291), an actual *Genuswechsel* is highly unlikely in this case, as no consistent transition or complete change to a new set of gender indicative modifiers in any one substantive could be identified in the analysed material.

As regards the absolute chronology of the restructuring process, the influence of the productive inflection can already be observed in the early Old English material with forms such as the genitive sg. *neahtes* or the nominative/accusative pl. *cȳe*, found in the text of *Vespasian Psalter* (PsGlA (Kuhn)), dated to the mid-9th century. Generally, however, the majority of innovative forms were found primarily in prose texts of Late West Saxon provenance. This applies to the influence of both strong and weak inflection, the latter attested predominantly in forms of the genitive pl. and nominative/accusative pl. (*-ana*, *-ena*, *-an*). With respect to gender variation, hardly any conclusive statement can be arrived at about the chronological or dialectal pattern of distribution of the novel forms. Traces of more explicit lack of gender agreement are to be found in the West-

Saxon material and the northern, 10th c. *Durham Ritual* (DurRitGl 1). In terms of dialectal distribution, most of the instances of innovative inflection were found scattered in the texts of West-Saxon provenance (in the late or intermediate period), and sporadic attestation of the innovative inflection was also identified in the late Anglian material (10th c.) (*Lindisfarne Gospels and Durham Ritual*).

The investigated material may not be sufficient to corroborate the existence of a temporary subsystem, as suggested originally by Jones (1967, 1988) for the period of late Old English, wherein case exists independently of gender (i.e., where overt function marking prevailed over overt gender marking), but it certainly displays characteristics of this stage (cf. Stenroos 2008). In view of the confusion present in the system of gender and case categories (brought about largely by phonological changes and the ensuing loss of inflectional distinctions), the inflectional markers could no longer carry the function of gender markers, and, consequently, the rules of the existing system had to be reinterpreted, resulting in the marginalisation of gender and the prevalence of functional/case marking (Jones 1988: 18). In other words, the earlier gender and case indicative function of inflections has, to some extent, been waived in favour of one purely of case, with all the remaining inflectional endings being interpreted as case markers without a gender distinction, as was made explicit by Millar (2002: 295): "...in order to preserve the function marker purpose of the forms and morphemes, their grammatical gender associations have been sacrificed". The process is well illustrated by the fate of the genitive sg. (with the distinctive -*es* marker), evident also in the pattern emergent from the present study, which in the early Middle English period emerged as the only independent and unambiguous case category in the singular. The development has been viewed in terms of a preventive measure against the disintegration of the original system, which seems to be consistent with Kuryłowicz's fifth law of analogy, whereby a central contrast (feature) is re-established at the expense of a marginal one, consequently eliminated (cf. "conservative radicalism", i.e., "the desire to retain as much as possible of the inherited system whilst reorganising and simplifying in order to remove ambiguity" (Millar 2002: 295, 302).[26] Consequently, the attested gender confusion manifested in the adoption of masculine inflectional markers in the feminine paradigm, found in the investigated data, should not be viewed as a proof of gender reclassification of the nouns, but as a development testifying to a gradual demise of the category of gender.

---

26 Compare the state of affairs in modern German where gender has been viewed as "an organizational principle in the development of inflection classes since Germanic" (Duke 2005: 45). The relationship between gender and declensional classes is much tighter than in English and the so called *Genusprofilierung* takes place (Wegera 1987), whereby "gender gains in importance as a criterion for the distribution of inflectional allomorphs", with a clear border line/opposition emerging between the masculine and neuter gender on the one hand, and feminine, on the other (Duke 2005: 43).

To conclude, the investigated material proves that the process of restructuring of the inflectional system was governed by gender-based analogy, whereby the interparadigmatic reshufflings were congruous with gender classes. The findings, though offering limited information about actual gender change, seem to comply with the principle of gender conservation in that the extension of novel inflection follows essentially the envisaged path of development. In order to obtain a more comprehensive picture of the restructuring of gender alongside the interparadigmatic reshufflings, it would be necessary and surely worth taking a closer look at some other minor inflectional classes, especially the unproductive vocalic declensions (the *i*-stems or *u*-stems), testifying to a much more advanced stage of inflectional disintegration, which may be consequential for the pattern of gender marking therein.

References

Adamczyk, Elżbieta
    2009   "Evolution of Germanic nominal inflection: The case of West Germanic kinship terms", *Sprachwissenschaft* 34: 398-433.
    in press "On morphological realignments in Old English root nouns", *Transactions of the Philological Society*.
Bammesberger, Alfred
    1990   *Die Morphologie des urgermanischen Nomens*. Heidelberg: Winter.
Baron, Naomi S.
    1971   "A reanalysis of Old English grammatical gender", *Lingua* 27: 113-140.
Blake, Norman
    1992   *The Cambridge history of the English language*. Vol. 2. *1066-1476*. Cambridge: Cambridge University Press.
Bosworth, Joseph (ed.)
    1898   *An Anglo-Saxon Dictionary*. (Supplement by T. Northcote Toller, Oxford, 1921; addenda and corrigenda by Alistair Campbell, Oxford, 1972). Oxford: Clarendon Press.
Brunner, Karl
    1965   *Altenglische Grammatik. Nach der angelsächsischen Grammatik von Eduard Sievers*. (3rd edition.) Tübingen: Niemeyer.
Bybee, Joan L.
    1985   *Morphology. A study of the relation between form and meaning*. (Typological Studies in Language 9). Amsterdam/Philadelphia: John Benjamins Publishing Company.
Bybee, Joan L. – Paul Hopper
    2001   "Introduction to frequency and the emergence of linguistic structure", in: Joan L. Bybee – Paul Hopper (eds.), 1-24.

Bybee, Joan L. – Paul Hopper (eds.)
2001   *Frequency and the emergence of linguistic structure.* Amsterdam: John
          Benjamins Publishing Company.
Cameron, Angus
1973   "A list of Old English texts", in: Roberta Frank – Angus Cameron (eds.),
          25-306.
Campbell, Alistair
1959   *Old English grammar.* Oxford: Clarendon Press.
Clark Cecily
1957   "Gender in the Peterborough Chronicle 1070-1154", *English Studies* 38:
          109-115.
Coleman, Fran
2008   "Names, derivational morphology, and Old English gender", *Studia
          Anglica Posnaniensia* 44: 29-52.
Corbett, Greville
1991   *Gender.* Cambridge: Cambridge University Press.
Curzan, Anne
2003   *Gender shifts in the history of English.* Cambridge: Cambridge University
          Press.
Duke, Janet
2005   "Gender systems and grammaticalization: Examples from German and
          Germanic", in: Torsten Leuschner et al. (eds.), 31-58.
Eaton, Roger – Olga Fischer – Willem F. Koopman – Frederike van der Leek (eds.)
1985   *Papers from the 4th International Conference on English Historical
          Linguistics (ICEHL), Amsterdam, April 10–13, 1985.* (Current Issues in
          Linguistic Theory 41.) Amsterdam: John Benjamins.
Fisiak, Jacek (ed.)
1980   *Historical morphology.* The Hague: Mouton de Gruyter.
2002   *Studies in English historical linguistics and philology: A Festschrift for
          Akio Oizumi.* (Studies in English Medieval Language and Literature 2.)
          Bern: Peter Lang.
Frank, Roberta – Angus Cameron (eds.)
1973   *A plan for the Dictionary of Old English.* Toronto: University of Toronto
          Press.
Griepentrog, Wolfgang
1995   *Die Wurzelnomina des Germanischen und ihre Vorgeschichte.* Innsbruck:
          Innsbrucker Beiträge zur Sprachwissenschaft.

Hall, Clark J. R.
1960   *A concise Anglo-Saxon dictionary.* (4th edition.) Cambridge: Cambridge
          University Press.
Healey, Antonette di Paolo (ed.)
2004   *The Dictionary of Old English corpus in electronic form.* Toronto:
          Toronto University Press.

Hogg, Richard M.
1992   "Phonology and morphology", in: Richard Hogg (ed.), 67-167.
1997   "Some remarks on case marking in Old English", *Transactions of the Philological Society* 95: 95-109.
Hogg, Richard M. (ed.)
1992   *The Cambridge history of the English language.* Vol. 1. *The beginnings to 1066.* Cambridge: Cambridge University Press.
Jones, Charles
1967   "The functional motivation of linguistic change", *English Studies* 48: 97-111.
1988   *Grammatical gender in English: 950-1250.* London: Croom Helm.
Kastovsky, Dieter
2000   "Inflectional classes, morphological restructuring, and the dissolution of Old English grammatical gender", in: Barbara Unterbeck et al. (eds.), 709-28.
Kärre Karl
1915   *Nomina agentis in Old English. Part 1. Introduction.* Uppsala: Uppsala University Press.
Keyser, Samuel Jay – Wayne O'Neil
1985   "The simplification of the Old English strong nominal paradigms", in: Roger Eaton et al. (eds.), 85-107.
Kitson, Peter
1990   "On Old English nouns of more than one gender", *English Studies* 71: 185-221.
Krygier, Marcin
2002   "A re-classification of Old English nouns", *Studia Anglica Posnaniensia* 38: 311-319.
Lahiri, Aditi – Bezalel Elan Dresher
1983   "Diachronic and synchronic implications of declension shifts", *Linguistic Review* 3: 141-164.
Lass, Roger
1992   "Phonology and morphology", in: Norman Blake (ed.), 23-155.
1997   "Why *house* is an Old English 'masculine *a*-stem'?", in: Terttu Nevalainen – Leena Kahlas-Tarkka (eds.), 101-109.
Leiss, Elisabeth
2000   "Gender in Old High German", in: Barbara Unterbeck et al. (eds.), 237-258.
Leuschner, Torsten – Tanja Mortelmans – Sarah De Groodt (eds.)
2005   *Grammatikalisierung im Deutschen.* Berlin/New York: Mouton de Gruyter.
Millar, Robert McColl
2002   "After Jones: Some thoughts on the final collapse of the grammatical gender system in English", in: Jacek Fisiak (ed.), 293-306.
Mitchell, Bruce
1986   *Old English syntax.* Oxford: Clarendon Press.

Nevalainen, Terttu – Leena Kahlas-Tarkka (eds.)
1997   *To explain the present*: *Studies in the changing English language in honour of Matti Rissanen*. (Mémoires de la Société Néophilologique de Helsinki 52.) Helsinki: Société Néophilologique.
Quirk, Randolph – Charles Leslie Wrenn
1957   *An Old English grammar*. London: Methuen.
Ross, Alan S.C.
1936   "Sex and gender in the Lindisfarne Gospels", *Journal of English and Germanic Philology* 35: 321-330.
Rumble, Alexander R. – David Mills (eds.)
1997   *Names, places and people: An onomastic miscellany in memory of John McNeal Dodgson*. Stamford: Paul Watkins.
Sandred, Karl Inge
1991   "Nominal inflection in the Old English of the Anglo-Saxon land charters: Change of gender or analogy?", *Studia Neophilologica* 63: 3-12.
1997   "Reading a Kentish charter", in: Alexander R. Rumble – David Mills (eds.), 320 325.
Schenker, Walter
1971   "*-es/-os-* Flexion und *-es/-os-* Stämme im Germanischen", *Beiträge zur Geschichte der deutschen Sprache und Literatur* 93: 46-59.
Steinmetz, Donald
2006   "Gender shifts in Germanic and Slavic: Semantic motivation for neuter?", *Lingua* 116: 1418-1440.
Stenroos, Merja
2008   "Order out of chaos? The English gender change in the Southwest Midlands as a process of semantically based reorganization", *English Language and Linguistics* 12: 445-473.
Toller, Thomas Northcote (ed.)
1921   *An Anglo-Saxon Dictionary. Supplement*. Oxford: Clarendon Press.
Unterbeck, Barbara – Matti Rissanen – Terttu Nevalainen – Mirja Saari (eds.)
2000   *Gender in grammar and cognition*. (Trends in Linguistics. Studies and Monographs 124.) Berlin/New York: Mouton de Gruyter.
Wełna, Jerzy
1980   "On gender change in linguistic borrowing", in: Jacek Fisiak (ed.), 399-420.
1996   *English historical morphology*. Warszawa: Wydawnictwo Uniwersytetu Warszawskiego.
Wegera, Klaus-Peter
1987   *Flexion der Substantive*. Vol. 3 of Hugo Moser – Hugo Stopp – Werner Besch (eds.), *Grammatik des Frühneuhochdeutschen. Beiträge zur Laut- und Formenlehre*. Heidelberg: Winter.

The chronological width in the *OED* reconstruction of Middle English verbs and derivatives

Michael Bilynsky, Ivan Franko National University of Lviv, Ukraine

ABSTRACT

The earliest quotations of words attested in the *Oxford English Dictionary* are conducive to a reconstruction of diachronic relationships in the lexicon. The software-sustainable queries to sets of homogeneously dated (timed in the same year or put within an arbitrary or database-conditioned 'natural' threshold of temporal convergence) or heterogeneously dated (with a one-year differential or arbitrary age divergence values) shared-root verbs and suffix- uniform/variant coinages reveal measures of the chronological *width* within the word forming families. The chronological width in the two-member sequences of the verb and a coinage is tantamount to the age differential of the respective textual prototypes. For sequences containing more than two constituents the chronological width is a crude estimation of the diachronic paths of shared-root word formation over time which involves precedent/following variedly outlying diachronic positioning. The on-site queries to the developed electronic system can be accompanied with an exemplary or exhaustive downloading of the factual evidence and re-settable diagram visualization.

Preliminary remarks

Coining a deverbal derivative consists in attaching a suffix to the parent verb at some point of time. It is reflected in its earliest textual citation. The appearance of the verb is documented in its textual prototype as well. The chronological relationship between the verbal base and its derivative can be threefold. There are verbs which had been in the lexicon prior to the first attestation of a deverbative. The earliest attestation of verbs could fall on the same time as that of at least one of their coinages. There are also verbs which were not attested at the time when the same-root coinage came to be recorded.

The deverbal word-formation entails the manifestations of substance and/or property related to the verb in the form of nouns and/or adjectives/participles. These constitute two branches of deverbal word forming families: substantivization and adjectivization. Understandably, within the latter adjectives are outnumbered by the lexicalized participles.

The process of the expansion of the lexicon is uneven owing to the varied speed of the actualization of the derivational potential of word forming bases and, consequently, the differences in the behaviour of derivational categories that are evinced in their diachronic productivity. Thus, the establishment of word forming relations can be reconstructed on the basis of the age of the lexemes involved in it.

In historical corpus linguistics the first attestation of a word is called its diachronic textual prototype. We can also take the text in which the earliest citation of a word occurs for its precedent text. Notwithstanding a certain amount of relativism in the dating, such a precedent text is by and large a reliable source of our knowledge of the time and sometimes the circumstances under which a word showed itself in the written medium of the language for the first time. The first quotations of the words in the *OED* make up a database of the textual evidence (Hoffmann 2004; cf., also Brewer 2004) supporting the appearance of the lexical-derivational inventory over time.

Classes of deverbal coinages

The categorization of nouns accepted here distinguishes between two groups of action nouns. The first group are those whose status as action nouns has remained intact in their *OED* listed meanings (d_1). In the second group alongside the meaning of action (d_2) a factitive (Kastovsky 1985) meaning ($d_{2'}$) can be found in the *OED* glosses. Action and factitve nouns shared the same set of suffixes in ME. The most productive action nouns formative is the primordial suffix *-ing* (e.g., *betoking* 1175). Several Romance suffixes (*-ance/-ence, -ment, -tion/-sion -age, -ure, -al, -y*) in the ME sources are less productive or even sporadic (e.g., *annoyance* 1386, *devisement* 1325, *conversion* 1340, *coverture* 1393, *deposal* 1397, *repassage* 1433, *inquiry* 1440). The imposed chronological limitation may contribute to the fact that only one of the action/factitive meanings of a noun is registered for ME. For instance, *devisement* in the meaning of the action noun (d_2) is registered in the *OED* in 1325 whereas in that of the factitive noun ($d_{2'}$) only in 1541. Conversely, the noun *elevation* offers its earliest *OED* attestation in the factitve sense ($d_{2'}$) in 1391 and as an action noun (d_2) in 1526.

Here and further on all examples are given in contemporary spelling. The asterisk after the lexeme denotes that it is registered in the *OED* as archaic.

The second major class of deverbal nouns are those denoting a source of the verbal action (d_3). Most typically, they signify the agent of the action but not infrequently also another deep case such as the instrument and/or force or, occasionally, just the latter deep case(s) alone (Dalton-Puffer 1994). For the sake of convenience we will refer to such nouns as agent nouns. These had several suffixes, the most typical of which was the Germanic *-er* with the earliest *ME* coinage *robber* attested in 1175. The Romance formative *-or* (e.g., *confessor* 1300) is much less productive than the formative *-er* whereas the other (most of them borrowed) suffixes were numerically insignificant. The suffixes *-ant* and *-ive* (e.g., *defendant* 1314, *digestive* 1386) were quite rare. Each of nounal suffixes *-ar, -ard, -and, -ster* and *-ory* reveals only one *ME* coinage registered in the *OED*: *beggar* 1225, *pursuand** 1300, *sluggard* 1398, *browdster** 1450, *distillatory* 1460. The nouns in the borrowed suffix *-ee* (d_4) for denoting the deep case of patient and also sometimes that of the object (e.g., *assignee* 1419, *feoffee* 1411, *ordinee* 1330, *presentee* 1429) were quite rare. Sporadically, they took up the suffixes of the agent nouns.

In deverbal adjectivization ($d_5 - d_8$) the calculus proceeds from the adjective to the participle and from the active diathesis to the passive one also marked by the category of modality.

The studied corpus of the present participle (d_6) consists predominantly of the coinages with the primordial *-ing* formative though in a proportion of the *OED* lemmas the precedent text has a coinage with its *OE* counterpart in *-nt/-nd*. The forms of past participles (d_8) are in the primordial *-ed* with the only participial borrowing from French in *-ee* (e.g., *ordinee* 1330) and nine lexicalized forms of participles of the types of *withholden* 1430 and *overthought** 1250. Modal deverbal adjectives (d_7) had the borrowed suffixes. Typically they ended in *-able* (e.g., *departable* 1483), sometimes in *-ible* (e.g., *convertible* 1386). The greatest variance of the formative can be seen in deverbal adjectives (d_5). The majority of them were borrowed. Most of the coinages were formed by means of the suffixes *-ive* (e.g., *mitigative* 1400) and *-ant* (e.g., *conversant* 1340) but some with the help of the suffixes *-ous, -ent, -and* or *-ory* (e.g., *desirous* 1300, *precedent* 1391, *preparatory* 1413). The two primordial adjectival suffixes *-ful* and *-y* as in, e.g., *praiseful* 1382, *droopy* 1225, were of low productivity. The adjectival *-and* formative built up only several now archaic *ME* coinages: *pursuand** 1390; *obeisand** 1375; *pearand** 1375; *suffiand** 1456; *prochand**1470.

Morphonemically, the coinage and the base sometimes, as in e.g., *prepare* ... *preparatory*, may fail to meet the requirement of transparency which does not refute their ultimate relatedness.

All the coinages taken into account in this study were specifically checked for their relatedness to the verbal base. The relatedness was accepted as established on condition of documented *OED* evidence. This is especially significant for the cases where the base of a coinage (e.g., *desirous* 1300, *praiseful*, 1382) alongside of the verb, as documented here, could also be the noun with the respective coincident or different dating.

In most cases the earliest attestation of a lexeme is given in the *OED* clearly. The approximations marked by the *OED* compilers by *about* and *circa*, as in *lisp a* 1100 and *weeder c* 1440 were entered into the calculus by the given dates. Century dating, e.g., 13.. as in *display 13..* was extended to the next *OED* attestation, *display* 1320, or, failing that, to the last year of the century, e.g., *staking 13..*, 1399. In the rare cases of period dating, e.g. *procession* 1103-23, the earlier date was processed.

Within the studied categorial types of deverbatives there are instances of synonymous suffixes attached to the same stem. When focusing on the categories expressed by variant suffixes the older counterpart was entered into the main base. Naturally, electronic modelling allows for the splitting of the main base by the variant suffix(es) within an agreed category.

When an action noun was coined by a suffix and another one coined by a synonymous suffix was lexicalized into a factitive noun ($d_{2'}$) they were imputed to different slots of the framework (d_1 and d_2). Alternatively, at their aggregate calculus ($d_{1/2}$) the precedent action noun coinage (d_1 or d_2), whether or not relating to the factitive countepart ($d_{2'}$), was counted for the filled-in position. At the suffix variance of factitive nouns ($d_{2'}$) an earlier counterpart was taken into account irrespective of whether it was a lexicalization of the action noun (d_2) or an independent derivative (also ascribed to $d_{2'}$).

When the suffix-variant coinages were dated in the same year the one with a more (eventually, at more than two variants, most) productive suffix was taken as the precedent form.

Discussion

The age difference between the first attestation of the verb and that of its derivative reveals the duration over which the respective lexeme existed in the lexicon without its counterpart. This time lag is understood as the *historical time factor* of the lexeme. In the course of this time the older member of the would-be relationship existed without its prospective younger counterpart. Thus, the historical time factor stands for the temporary, i.e., pre-combinatorial (and pre-paradigmatic) existence of the older member of a pair of words. At the positive value of the age difference and a genuine word-forming relationship between the verb and its derivative the said factor characterizes the time taken by the lexicon to create a coinage – tentatively, the *transpositional time of the coinage*. When the derivative is older than its verbal base the respective historical time factor reflects the *reverse transpositional time* of the coinage manifested in the back derivation of its base, potentially contributive to the study of the processes of delexicalization.

The historical time factor value is in most cases a fact from the history of the language since the morphemically marked structure of the derivative was conducive to its being conspicuous in the texts analyzed for the *OED*. In view of the known strategy of the *OED* compilers to look for new unusual words appearing over time the registration of coinages was generally accurate (Brewer 1993: 321). Some observations concerning the likelihood of the antedating in different classes of deverbatives are found in (Schäfer 1989: 59, 67-68).

The ME lexicon is marked by the interaction of the borrowed Romance and primordial Germanic elements. The borrowed verbs took on both borrowed and primordial transpositional formatives. The Germanic verbs took on the borrowed suffixes in Middle English too rarely to produce enough evidence for this study. The primordial bases derivationally active in ME with respect to the Germanic suffixes could be registered in the *OED* textual prototypes within the period (1150-1500) and also before it (prior to 1150).

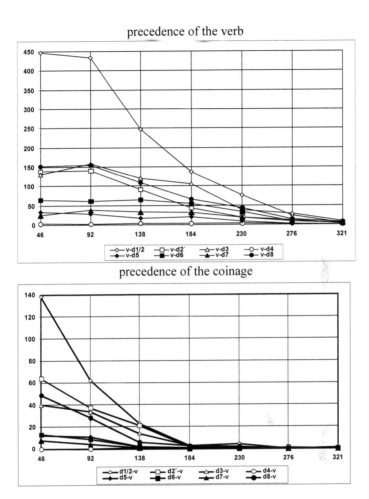

Figure 1. Distribution of the age differential values between the earliest *OED* attestations for ME verbs and their shared-root derivatives: axis *x* – the scopes of the age differential in years: axis *y* – number of cases. Symbol notations: v – verb; $d_{1/2}$ – non-lexicalized or lexicalizable (according to the precedent form) aggregate calculus of action nouns; d_2· – factitive nouns; d_3 – nouns denoting a source (agent or instrument) of the action; d_4 – patient nouns, d_5 – adjectives; d_6 – lexicalized present participles; d_7 – modal adjectives; d_8 – lexicalized past participles (same as on the charts below).

In shared-root verb-deverbative pairs with the positive (verb first) or negative (derivative first) age differential between the *OED* textual prototypes a certain number of examples (axis y on Fig. 1) falls for an interval of values of the age differential of textual prototypes expressed in years (axis x on Fig 1). Understandably, the negative age differential of the textual prototypes of verb-deverbative pairs occurs less frequently than the positive values of the temporal difference between them. Also, the values of the chronological width between the verb and its derivative at the positive age differential tended to be generally larger than those at the negative difference between them. Hence, the curves reflecting the positive values of the temporal differential (deverbative second) are generally flatter than the ones for its negative values (verb second).

The presented processing of the chronologically diverse factual evidence can be regarded as relevant should the analyzed categories reveal discrepancies with respect to the distribution of the values of the age difference between the first attestations of the compared categories. The relevance will be also there, if there is more similarity between some categories than between others.

As can be seen from Figure 1 in aggregate action nouns ($d_{1/2}$) the chronologically least heterogeneous textual prototypes of the verb and coinage (extreme left hand-side point on the curves) fall on approximately one third of the cases with the precedent coinage and two thirds of the cases with the precedent verb. Factitive ($d_{2'}$) and agent (d_3) nouns as well as past participles (d_8) reveal almost convergent curvature of the distribution of the age differential values when the coinage follows the verb. In the opposite case, when the verb follows the coinage the respective distribution curves are divergent.

The prerequisite for the material to be included into this study lay in the availability of both the verb and its coinage(s) in the textual prototypes attested within the ME period. As most of the verbs of native etymology as the potential bases for word formation in ME were attested before the start of this period, i.e., still during Old English, the studied coinages were to a considerable extent (see below) related to verbs of Romance etymology.

Being followed by the suffixes of Romance etymology these bases produced a distribution of the age differential between the diachronic textual prototypes that was quite divergent from that revealed by the ME verbal bases at large (cf. Fig. 2 and 1). A notable point of difference is a more proportional representation of the factitive nouns ($d_{2'}$) and action nouns ($d_{1/2}$), especially in the cases when the verb was younger than its factitive derivative. Thus, we see almost convergent curves 1 and 2 on Fig. 2 in contrast to their counterparts on Fig. 1. Besides this, there was also a notable drop in the agent nouns (d_3) and an interesting interplay of the factual productivity and chronological distance from the base between classes of adjectives (cf. curves 5 and 6 on Fig. 2).

precedence of the Romance etymology verb

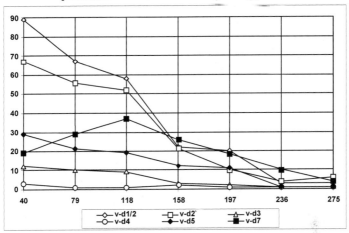

precedence of the derivative

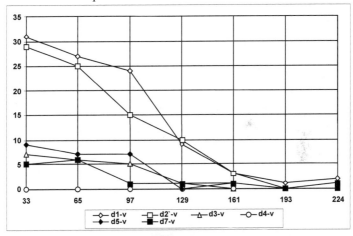

Figure 2. Distribution of the age differential values between the earliest *OED* attestations for ME verbs of Romance etymology and their shared-root derivatives.

In action and agent nouns from the verbs of Romance etymology the Germanic formatives *-ing* and *-er* were more productive than their Romance etymology counterparts. Conversely, the Romance suffixes were more productive within factitive nouns than the primordial suffix *-ing* (cf. Fig. 2 and 1).

44   M. Bilynsky

When the Romance bases took on primordial formatives (Fig. 3) the respective curvatures almost (with the exception of the correlation between the factitive nouns ($d_{2'}$) and past participles (d_8) in both patterns of precedence) coincide with the average ones (Fig. 1).

precedence of the Romance etymology verb

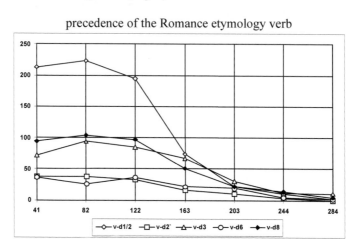

precedence of the derivative

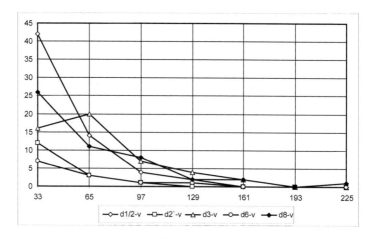

Figure 3. Distribution of the age differential values between the earliest *OED* attestations for ME verbs of Romance etymology and shared-root derivatives with Germanic suffixes.

When the native suffix was attached to the verbs of Germanic etymology in ME the curve for the aggregate action nouns remains predominant as in the total selection (cf. Fig. 4 and 1). Other curves fail to reveal groupings in productivity. The lexicalization of action nouns into same-word factitive counterparts was quite uncommon (cf. curve 2 in Fig. 1 and 4).

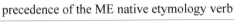

precedence of the ME native etymology verb

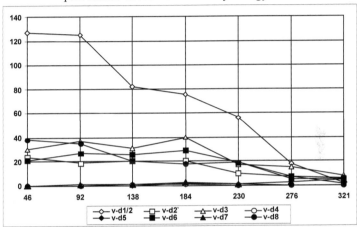

precedence of the derivative

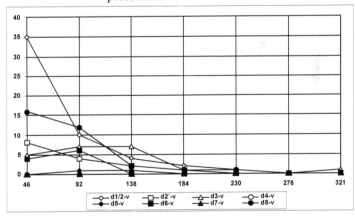

Figure 4. Distribution of the age differential values between the earliest *OED* attestations for ME verbs of Germanic etymology and shared-root derivatives with the Germanic suffixes.

The above visualization juxtaposes the predominant follow-up of the derivative after the verb (upper curves) with the instances when the derivative precedes the verb. Pointing out the examples *burglar* 1265 *vs. to burgle* 1872 Kastovsky (2000: 121) offers to speak about the analyzability of a derivative rather than its motivation (cf., also, Strang 1970). For space considerations we will limit our exemplification to the exhaustive download of ME agent nouns preceding the verb although each deverbal category revealed a certain share of cases of the precedent verb in respect to the derivative (cf. lower charts on Fig. 1-4).

Examples grouped by: d3; v

-adulter* 1382, adulterer 1370(3)
-alterate* 1475, alterative 1398(3)
-approve 1483, approver* 1386(3)
-arbitre* 1494, arbitrer* 1382(3)
-armour 1450, armourer 1386(3)
-assess 1447, assessor 1380(3)
-assize* 1393, assizer 1330(3)
-battle 1330, battler 1300(3)
-botch 1382, botcher 1375(3)
-brag 1377, bragger 1362(3)
-brawde* 1483, brawdster* 1450(3)
-broider* 1450, broiderer 1388(3)
-broke 1496, broker 1377(3)
-cap 1483, capper 1389(3)
-caulk 1500, caulker 1495(3)
-chant 1386, chanter 1297(3)
-chinch* 1440, chincher* 1386(3)
-chronicle 1440, chronicler 1387(3)
-cobble 1496, cobbler 1362(3)
-comment 1450, commenter 1387(3)
-compile 1375, compiler 1330(3)
-confess 1340, confessor 1300(3)
-control 1475, controller 1393(3)
-counsel 1290, counsellor 1225(3)
-create 1386, creator 1290(3)
-crucifix* 1483, crucifixer* 1450(3)
-dag* 1400, dagger 1386(3)
-detract 1449, detractor 1382(3)
-digest 1450, digestive 1386(3)
-divine 1362, diviner 1330(3)
-elect 1494, elector 1467(3)
-embroider 1420, embroiderer 1413(3)
-enchant 1374, enchanter 1297(3)
-encheat* 1460, encheater* 1387(3)
-extortion 1494, extortioner 1375(3)
-farm 1440, farmer 1385(3)
-forage 1417, forager 1377(3)
-foray 1375, forayer 1330(3)

-forespeak 1300, forespeaker* 1175(3)
-grate 1420, grater 1390(3)
-hostel 1330, hosteler 1290(3)
-image 1440, imager 1399(3)
-instruct 1477, instructor 1460(3)
-invade 1491, invasor* 1443(3)
-labour 1362, labourer 1325(3)
-lax 1398, laxative 1386(3)
-lecher* 1382, lecherer* 1380(3)
-limit 1380, limiter 1377(3)
-limn 1440, limner 1389(3)
-load 1495, loader 1476(3)
-malign 1426, maligner 1425(3)
-medicine 1450, mediciner 1375(3)
-enchant 1374, enchanter 1297(3)
-encheat* 1460, encheater* 1387(3)
-extortion 1494, extortioner 1375(3)
-farm 1440, farmer 1385(3)
-forage 1417, forager 1377(3)
-foray 1375, forayer 1330(3)
-forespeak 1300, forespeaker* 1175(3)
-grate 1420, grater 1390(3)
-hostel 1330, hosteler 1290(3)
-image 1440, imager 1399(3)
-instruct 1477, instructor 1460(3)
-invade 1491, invasor* 1443(3)
-labour 1362, labourer 1325(3)
-lax 1398, laxative 1386(3)
-lecher* 1382, lecherer* 1380(3)
-limit 1380, limiter 1377(3)
-limn 1440, limner 1389(3)
-load 1495, loader 1476(3)
-malign 1426, maligner 1425(3)
-medicine 1450, mediciner 1375(3)
-mine 1330, miner 1275(3)
-moderate 1432, moderator 1398(3)
-mollify 1412, mollificative* 1400(3)
-mucker 1374, muckerer* 1303(3)

-peal 1400, pealer 1393(3)
-pepper 1500, pepperer 1180(3)
-pike 1463, piker 1301(3)
-possess 1465, possessor 1388(3)
-practise 1389, practiser* 1377(3)
-prison 1300, prisoner 1250(3)
-raven 1494, ravener 1374(3)
-regrate 1467, regrator 1362(3)
-rememorate* 1460, rememorative* 1424(3)
-rifle 1352, rifler 1326(3)
-ring 1499, ringer 1425(3)
-rob 1225, robber 1175(3)
-romance 1399, romancer 1338(3)
-rounge* 1375, rounger* 1338(3)
-scum 1380, scummer 1326(3)
-slat 1475, slatter 1379(3)
-slive 1399, sliver 1374(3)
-slug 1425, sluggard 1398(3)

-solicit 1429, solicitor 1412(3)
-suppowell* 1400, suppoweller* 1391(3)
-survey 1467, surveyor 1440(3)
-tail 1315, tailor 1297(3)
-tallage 1460, tallager 1400(3)
-tassel 1366, tasseller 1301(3)
-tile 1375, tiler 1300(3)
-tipple 1500, tippler 1396(3)
-toll 1467, toller* 1313(3)
-tourney 1390, tourneyer 1303(3)
-trench 1483, trencher 1330(3)
-tun 1430, tunner 1337(3)
-ventose* 1400, ventoser* 1340(3)
-versify 1377, versifier 1340(3)
-whisk 1480, whisker 1425(3)
-woad 1464, woader 1415(3)
-wreche* 1330, wrecher* 1325(3)
-wrob* 1425, wrobber* 1300(3)

However, the suggested visualization did not include the list of instances of the same year dating of the textual prototypes of the compared categories (here as above exemplified by the ME agent nouns and their same-root verbs):

Examples grouped by: v, d3
-account 1303, accounter* 1303(3)
-adjure 1382, adjurer 1382(3)
-alarge* 1380, alarger* 1380(3)
-amble 1386, ambler 1386(3)
-bat-fowl 1440, bat-fowler 1440(3)
-beg 1225, beggar 1225(3)
-besom 1400, besomer 1400(3)
-burl 1483, burler 1483(3)
-burt* 1440, burter 1440(3)
-catechize 1449, catechizer 1449(3)
-cervylle* 1483, cervyller 1483(3)
-chase 1300, chaser 1300(3)
-consoude* 1400, consouder* 1400(3)
-cord 1430, corder 1430(3)
-demember 1491, demembrer 1491(3)
-discover 1300, discoverer 1300(3)
-drote* 1440, droter* 1440(3)
-ensearch 1382, ensearcher* 1382(3)
-evangelize 1382, evangelizer 1382(3)
-expulse* 1432, expulsor* 1432(3)
-fickle* 1225, fickler 1225(3)
-forhill* 1300, forhiller 1300(3)
-gender 1382, genderer 1382(3)
-globbe* 1377, globber 1377(3)

-glusk* 1440, glusker* 1440(3)
-grutch 1225, grutcher* 1225(3)
-guarish* 1474, guarisher* 1474(3)
-heckle 1440, heckler 1440(3)
-horn 1421, horner 1421(3)
-jape 1362, japer 1362(3)
-juffle* 1500, juffler* 1500(3)
-knack 1380, knacker 1380(3)
-lope 1483, loper 1483(3)
-malt 1440, malter 1440(3)
-nite* 1300, niter 1300(3)
-notify 1374, notifier 1374(3)
-ordain 1290, ordainer 1290(3)
-policy* 1450, policier* 1450(3)
-pop 1386, popper 1386(3)
-prate 1420, prater 1420(3)
-preach 1225, preacher 1225(3)
-provoke 1432, provoker 1432(3)
-punish 1340, punisher 1340(3)
-quoit 1440, quoiter 1440(3)
-ransom 1300, ransomer 1300(3)
-recure* 1382, recurer* 1382(3)
-reed 1440, reeder 1440(3)
-report 1386, reporter 1386(3)

-rest 1440, rester* 1440(3)   -trip 1380, tripper 1380(3)
-runk* 1460, runker* 1460(3)   -underplant 200, underplanter* 1200(3)
-shovel 1440, shoveller 1440(3)   -violate 1432, violator 1432(3)
-shrag* 1440, shragger* 1440(3)   -voyage 1477, voyager 1477(3)
-supplant 1300, supplanter 1300(3)   -web 1440, webber 1440(3)
-thrumble 1500, thrumbler* 1500(3)   -wharl 1440, wharler 1440(3)
-tilth 1495, tilther 1495(3)   -withtake* 1340, withtaker* 1340(3)
-tittle 1399, tittler* 1399(3)   -wrawl 1440, wrawler 1440(3)
-torment 1290, tormentor 1290(3)

The zero age differential between the textual prototypes of the verb and its derivative can be included into the general pattern of age differential values. Setting the optimal minimal number of intervals for the chronological evidence arising from the correlation of the verb with derived categories involves a better reflection of the concentration of individual values within an interval and, if available, the 'natural' breaches in the values on the border lines between the adjacent intervals (cf. the respective lines on the tables beside the charts on Fig. 5-6).

We call the area on the graph on either side of the zero differential that of diachronic *emergentism* of the respective verb and a derivation type. It appears that at the same number of intervals a derivational category may claim most of the available examples for the emergentism area (cf. the upper left hand-side chart on Fig. 5 and all but the lower right hand-side charts on Fig. 6) or for an area to the right of it (cf. the upper right hand-side chart on Fig. 6 and the lower left hand-side chart on Fig. 7). The interval with the highest concentration of the chronological evidence typically reaches both sides of the scale of the age differential values, though not necessarily in a symmetrical way. Alternatively, the same year textual prototypes of the verb and a derivation category may be the extreme value of an interval in the distribution of the chronological difference between the prototypes (cf. the lower chart on Fig. 5).

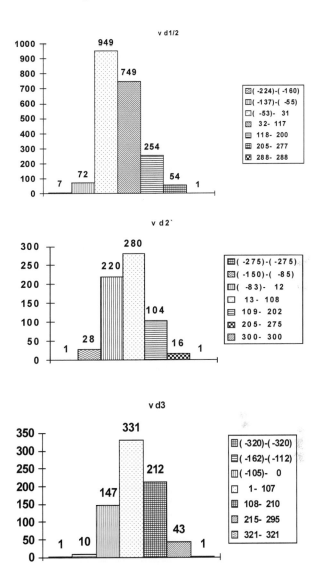

Figure 5. Integration of the same year dating of the verb and a derivation category into the distribution of the age differential values of ME verbs and substantives. Here and below symbol notations are the same as on Fig. 1 above.

M. Bilynsky

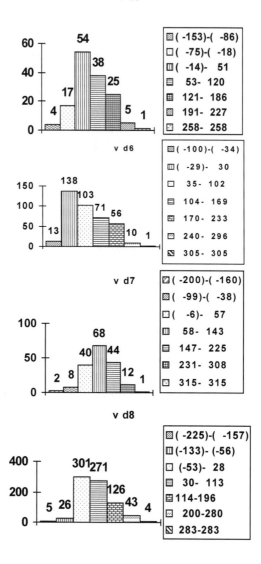

Figure 6. Integration of the same year dating of the verb and a derivation category into the distribution of the age differential values of ME verbs and adjectives or participles.

The etymological heterogeneity of the inventory of suffixes in deverbal nouns (highly productive -*Ing* and -*er* formatives against an array of Romance counterparts), unlike that of the suffixes involved in the re-categorizations of the process into a property with most Romance suffixes and only two (-*y* and -*full*) Germanic ones and of limited productivity) justifies the split modelling of the chronological heterogeneity of the textual prototypes compared. For the aggregate action nouns both precedent modelling and that split by the etymology of the involved suffixes basically preserve the balance of the distribution of age differential values (cf. the upper charts on Fig. 5 and 7-8). Factitive nouns, however, reveal a bend towards the emergentism area when the precedent coinage principle gave way to that of the etymological homogeneity of the suffix (cf. the second from the top charts on Fig.5 and 7-8). At the etymological uniformity of the suffix(es) of agent nouns the highest concentration of the chronological evidence falls on the area to the right of the emergentism interval (cf. the lower charts on Fig. 5 and 7-8).

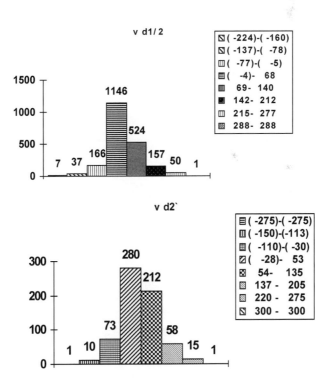

　　　　　　　　　　　M. Bilynsky

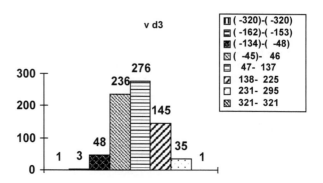

Figure 7. Integration of the same year dating of the verb and a derivation category into the distribution of the age differential values of ME verbs and substantives in -*ing* ($d_{1/2}$ and $d_{2'}$) and -*er* (d_3).

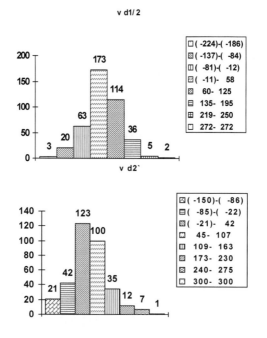

v d3

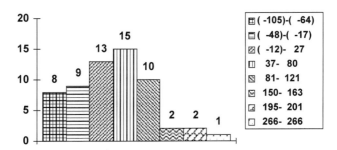

Figure 8. Integration of the same year dating of the verb and a derivation category into the distribution of the age differential values of ME verbs and substantives in a precedent Romance suffix.

For a two-constituent sequence the temporal differential of age values distribution is tantamount to its chronological width (cf. below as an exemplification the action nouns in *-ing* (d_2) that have the same-word (sometimes post-ME) factitive counterpart ($d_{2'}$) and the action nouns of the same kind with a precedent Romance suffix on Fig. 9-10). The factual material within an interval is downloadable from the developed framework. Understandably, the intervals of the chronological heterogeneity in these two ways of accessing the same data do not coincide. For instance, the values of interval 4 on the lower graph on Fig. 9 (cf. the respective verb-derivative pairs below) stay within intervals 5-6 on the upper graph:

v d2

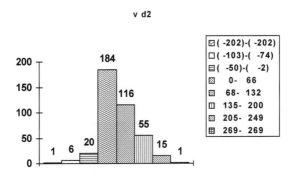

v d2

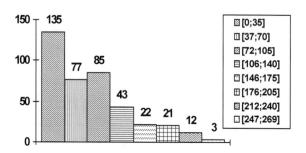

Figure 9. Integration of the same year dating of the verb and a derivation category into the distribution of the age differential values of ME verbs and lexicalizable action nouns (d$_2$) in -*ing*.

43 records (4th row on the table beside the lower chart)
selected form(s): verb, action nouns (d$_2$) in -*ing*
delta t : [106; 140] years in the age difference of textual prototypes

buck* [drench, soak] (1377), bucking (1483)
couple (1225), coupling (1340)
cover [cover] (1275), covering (1400)
cull [select, pick] (1330), culling (1440)
cut (1275), cutting (1398)
double (1290), doubling (1398)
dress (1330), dressing (1440)
enamel (1325), enamelling (1449)
enlarge (1380), enlarging (1494)
enter (1250), entering (1385)
exceed (1374), exceeding (1480)
file [pollute;accuse] (1200), filing (1340)
graith (1200), graithing (1340)
grieve (1225), grieving (1340)
grub (1300), grubbing (1440)
lard (1330), larding (1440)
liken (1303), likening (1440)
loose (1225), loosing (1357)
mis-say (1225), mis-saying (1340)
pave (1310), paving (1426)
plane (1320), planing (1440)
plaster (1300), plastering (1440).

powder [mix,season] (1300), powdering (1440)
pronounce (1330), pronouncing (1451)
quicken (1300), quickening (1430)
record (1225), recording (1340)
render (1325), rendering (1440)
rive [tear or pull] (1275), riving (1400)
ruffle [spoil,roughen] (1300), ruffling (1440)
seize (1290), seizing (1400)
signify (1250), signifying (1382)
spell [read letter by lette] (1300), spelling (1440)
spurge* (1303), spurging* (1440)
stint (1200), stinting (1338)
suffer (1225), suffering (1340)
truss (1225), trussing (1340)
wage (1320), waging (1456)
welter (1300), weltering (1423)
wrap (1320), wrapping (1440)
sermon (1175), sermoning* (1300)
lain (1300), laining (1440)
tary* (1300), tarying* (1440)
fellowship (1374), fellowshipping, (1486)

Both -ing (398 coinages in ME) and a (precedent) Romance suffix (322 coinages) action nouns (d₂) that were to be lexicalized into the same-word factitive noun (d₂′) gave the total of just 713 cases of filled-in ME positions with the ME verb and a d₂ noun testifying to a low occurrence of inter-suffix variation involving the primordial suffix *-ing* in this class of nouns from ME verbs in ME.

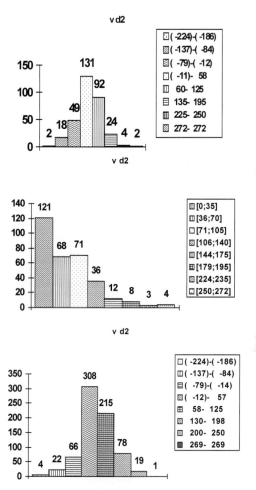

Figure 10. Integration of the same year dating of the verb and a derivation category into the distribution of the age differential values of ME verbs and lexicalizable action nouns (d₂) in a precedent Romance etymology suffix. The lower tier chart reflects the textual prototypes distribution between the shared-root verbs and lexicalizable action nouns (d₂) irrespective of the suffix.

M. Bilynsky

36 records of examples below (4th row on the table beside the medium chart)
selected form(s): verb, action nouns (d_2) in a (precedent) Romance suffix
delta t : [106; 140] years in the age difference of textual prototypes

accept (1360), acception (1483)	glorify (1340), glorification (1460)
adorn (1374), adornment (1480)	invent (1475), invention (1350)
alter (1374), alteration (1482)	labour (1362), labourage (1475)
annoy (1250), annoyance (1386)	multiply (1275), multiplication (1384)
appeach* (1315), appeachment* (1450)	obey (1290), obeyance (1400)
attach (1330), attachment (1447)	ordain (1290), ordainment (1399)
convict (1366), conviction (1491)	perceive (1300), perceivance (1440)
cover [cover] (1275), coverture (1393)	persecute (1477), persecution (1340)
crown (1175), crownment (1297)	possess (1465), possession (1340)
decide (1380), decision (1490)	predestinate (1450), predestination (1340)
descend (1300), descension(1420)	renounce (1375), renouncement (1494)
despair (1340), desperance (1225)	represent (1375), representation (1483)
determine (1374), determination (1483)	taint (1375), tainture (1490)
detract (1449), detraction (1340)	tarry (1320), tarriance (1460)
direct (1374), direction (1485)	transmute (1494), transmutation (1380)
disparage (1350), disparagement (1486)	dissever (1250), disseverance (1374)
embrace (1360), embracement (1485)	distil (1374), distillation (1499)
expose (1474), exposition (1340)	indign* (1490), indignation (1374)

For sequences containing more than two constituents the chronological width is a crude estimation (cf. the results of a sample query under Fig. 11 below) of the diachronic expansion of shared-root derivation over time which involves patterns of precedent/following variedly outlying positioning (cf. the upper and lower charts on Fig. 11). In the prevailing patterns of the diachronic expansion of such shared-root coinages with the precedent verb the concluding lag of positioning is generally tighter than the initial lag (cf. curves 1 and 3 with curves 2 and 4, respectively). This assumption is still to be checked on other sequences of shared-root verbs and their derivatives.

v d1/2 d3

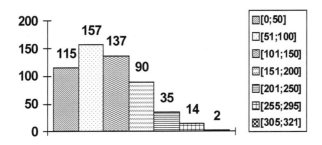

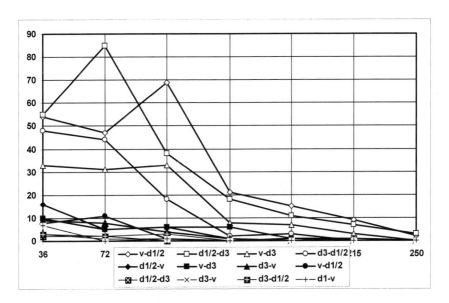

Figure 11. Chronological width of the diachronic positioning of the shared-root ME verbs, aggregate action nouns ($d_{1/2}$) and agent nouns (d_3).

35 records (5th row on the table beside the upper chart on Fig. 11)
selected form(s): verb, aggregate action nouns (d$_{1/2}$), agent noun (d$_3$)
delta t: [201; 251] years in the age difference of textual prototypes

betray (1250), betraying (1382), betrayer (1470)
big (1200), bigging* (1250), bigger (1440)
bolt [sift,pass thr.sieve] (1200), bolting (1300), bolter (1440)
breve* (1225), brevement* (1475), brever* (1475)
clip [cut with scissors] (1200), clipping (1440), clipper (1382)
clout (1225), clouting (1382), clouter (1440)
defoul (1290), defouling (1380), defouler (1499)
desire (1230), desiring (1377), desirer (1450)
dispute (1225), disputing (1225), disputer (1434)
elect (1494), election (1270), elector (1467)
excuse (1225), excusation (1300), excuser* (1461)
fawn [act slavishly] (1225), fawning (1225), fawner (1440)
gape (1220), gaping (1374), gaper (1470)
get (1200), getting (1398), getter (1440)
ground (1205), grounding (1380), grounder (1449)
haunt (1230), haunting (1325), haunter (1440)
judge (1225), judgement (1225), judger (1449)
kindle [set fire,ignite] (1200), kindling (1300), kindler (1450)
leese* [come to ruin] (1175), leesing* (1362), leeser* (1380)
mash [beat into soft mass] (1250), mashing (1399), masher (1500)
overset (1200), oversetting (1398), oversetter (1440)
paint (1250), painting (1497), painter (1340)
prove (1175), proving (1325), prover (1382)
quench (1200), quenching (1220), quencher (1440)
record (1225), recording (1340), recorder (1426)
rob (1225), robbing (1377), robber (1175)
ruck [squat,coach,cover] (1225), rucking (1440), rucker (1399)
saw (1225), sawing (1440), sawer (1379)
suffer (1225), sufferance (1300), sufferer (1450)
toll [attract,entice,decoy] (1220), tolling (1225), toller (1440)
undertake (1200), undertaking (1425), undertaker (1382)
wall [furnish w.a wall] (1250), walling (1480), waller (1440)
war [make war upon] (1154), warring (1380), warrer (1225)
withdraw (1225), withdrawing (1315), withdrawer (1475)
mistrow* (1225), mistrowing* (1300), mistrower* (1456)

Conclusion

The juxtaposing of the chronologized textual prototypes of the *OED* for verbs and
deverbal coinages lays the empirical foundation for the diachronic textually
attested derivatology of English. Alongside of generalizing visualization of the
collected variedly sliced databases of examples of shared-root verbs and deverbal
categories the developed framework allows to access the exhaustive *OED*-based

evidence the whole heuristic potential of which is still to be incorporated into the diachronic studies of the English lexicon.

References

Brewer, Charlotte
    2000   "*OED* sources", in: Lynda Mugglestone (ed.): 40-58.
    2004   "The 'electronification' of the *Oxford English Dictionary*". *Dictionaries.*
        Journal of the Dictionary Society of North America 25, 1-43
Dalton-Puffer, Christiane
    1994   "Are Shakespeare's agent nouns different from Chaucer's? – On the
        dynamics of a derivational subsystem", in: Dieter Kastovsky (ed.): 45-57.
Fisiak, Jacek (ed.)
    1985   *Historical semantics. Historical word-formation. Trends in Linguistics.*
        Studies and monographs, 29. Berlin: Mouton.
Hoffmann, Sebastian
    2004   "Using the *OED* quotations database as a corpus – a linguistic appraisal"
        ICAME Journal 28, 17-30.
Kastovsky, Dieter
    1985   "Deverbal nouns in Old and Middle English: From stem-formation to
        word-formation", in: Jacek Fisiak (ed.): 221-261.
    2000   "Words and word-formation: Morphology in *OED*", in: Mugglestone
        (ed.): 110-125.
Kastovsky, Dieter (ed.)
    1994   *Studies in Early Modern English.* The Hague: Mouton de Gruyter.
Mugglestone, Lynda (ed.)
    2000   *Lexicography and the OED. Pioneers in the* untrodden *forest.* Oxford:
        Oxford University Press.
OED Oxford English Dictionary (Second Edition) on CD-ROM Version 3.0. Oxford:
        Oxford University Press.
Schäfer, Jurgen
    1989   *Early Modern English lexicography. Additions and corrections to the*
        OED. Oxford: Clarendon Press, 1989. 2 vols.
Strang, Barbara M. H.
    1970   "Aspects of the history of the –ER formative in English". *Transactions of*
        the Philological Society 1969: 1-30.

Dative resumptive pronouns in Old English *þe* relatives[1]

Artur Bartnik, Catholic University of Lublin

ABSTRACT

This paper offers an analysis of the syntactic properties of dative resumptive pronouns in Old English relative clauses. In the syntactic literature, resumptive pronouns are elements in a relative clause that appear in the position where we would expect a gap, often as processing artifacts (McCloskey 2006, Sells 1984). Although they are marginal in standard Modern English they are adequately represented in the Old English corpus, which suggests that they are well integrated into the grammatical system of Old English. Traditional studies (Fischer 1992, Traugott 1992, Visser 1963-1973, Mitchell 1985) argue that Old English resumptives are used because they indicate the case of the particle *þe*, which cannot express case itself. In this study we will show that there are other factors that determine the distribution of dative resumptives. In particular, the form of the resumptive pronoun is determined by its role in the lower clause rather than by its relationship with the relative pronoun (cf. Allen 1977). Thus verbs, prepositions and other structures such as the verb *beon* and the comparative of the adjective *leofran* require indirect (dative) objects. This is also supported by the fact that dative resumptives appear both in *þe* and *se þe* relatives.

1. Introduction

This paper offers an analysis of the syntactic properties of dative resumptive pronouns in *þe* relatives in Old English. Resumptive pronouns are elements that appear in the position where we would expect a gap. Thus, the Modern English relative clause in (1), which contains a resumptive pronoun, can be contrasted with example (2), where the pronoun is expected; therefore it does not exhibit resumption. Example (3) is a typical relative clause where the gap marks the position of the relativized constituent inside the relative clause:

(1)   There are guests *who* I am curious about what <u>they</u> are going to say[2]
       McCloskey (2006: 94)

(2)   Most people think *that* <u>they</u> have the right to a decent job
       McCloskey (2006: 94)

---

1   I would like to thank Prof. Adam Pasicki for his help with the data and the audience at the 9th Medieval English Studies Symposium (MESS) for their instructive criticism and comments, especially Dr Laura Wright (University of Cambridge) and Prof. Xavier Dekeyser (University of Antwerp/KU Leuven).
2   For convenience, resumptive pronouns are underlined and relativizers italicized.

(3)   There are guests *that* everyone wants to invite ____
       McCloskey (2006: 95)

Syntactically, this contrast is explained by the obligatory binding of a resumptive pronoun or a gap by an antecedent. In (1) and (3) both the elements are bound by the noun *guests*. Pronouns such as those in (2) can find their binder in the discourse (cf. McCloskey 2006: 95).

Resumptive pronouns are considered marginal in Modern English. Their distribution is limited since they occur in contexts in which a gap would be ungrammatical or very difficult to process. Consider examples (4) and (5) below:

(4)   The book *that* I was wondering whether I should sue the author who wrote it
       Bondaruk (1995: 31)
(5a)   *This is the camel *that* he likes Oscar
(5b)   ?This is the camel *that* maybe, maybe, maybe, maybe he likes Oscar
(5c)   This is the camel *that* I think he likes Oscar
       McKee and McDaniel (2001: 114)

In (4) the resumptive pronoun *it* is used within the complex NP to save the sentence from island violations. In (5) the acceptability rises as the sentence becomes more complex. This is so because the further the head NP stands from the relativized item the harder it gets for the language user to establish the relation between the two constituents. A resumptive pronoun always facilities this task.

There are languages, however, in which resumptive strategies are not peripheral. On the contrary, resumptive pronouns are fully grammatical and seem to alternate with gaps in many syntactic contexts. Irish is a case in point:

(6)   an ghirseach *ar* ghoid na síogaí í
       the girl   C stole the fairies her
       'the girl who the fairies stole'
       McCloskey (2006: 95)

Sells (1984) labels resumption in English-type languages intrusive and in Irish-type languages true resumption. It is not easy to state unequivocally which group Old English belongs to. On the one hand, Visser (1963-1973 §75) claims that resumptive constructions are not uncommon[3], on the other hand Mitchell (1985 §2198) reports that such constructions appear in less than five per cent of *þe* clauses in prose, though they are unlikely to be archaic. At any rate, the fact that resumption existed in writing argues against the hypothesis that it was marginal like in Modern English and restricted to informal registers.

---

3   Of course, Visser does not use the term 'resumption', though his examples fit neatly into our analysis.

This paper offers a corpus analysis of resumption in *þe* relatives in Old English. We will analyse contexts in which dative resumptives are traditionally considered to be the most common. In section 2 we will give a brief overview of the literature on resumption in Old English. Section 3, the main body of the article, examines the grammatical contexts in which dative resumptives occur. Section 4 concludes the paper.

2. Previous studies on resumption in Old English

Generally, three major types of headed relative clauses can be distinguished in Old English. The most common type, the *þe* relative, was introduced by the indeclinable relative complementizer (cf. Allen 1980). This type is illustrated in (7). The other two types were introduced either by a relative pronoun (example 8) or a mixture of the complementizer *þe* and a relative pronoun (example 9).

(7)   Gemyne   he ðæs   yfeles   *þe*   he worhte
        Remember he the   evil   that he wrought
        'let him remember the evil that he wrought'
        CP Sweet 25.3, Allen (1980: 266)

(8)   Ac   ge   onfoð   ðæm mægene   Halges Gastes *se*   cymeð ofor   eow
        But   you   receive   the   power   Holy   Ghost who   comes over   you
        'but you shall receive the power of the Holy Ghost, who will come over you'
        Blickling 119. 11, Allen (1980: 269)

(9)   swa swa Aaron   wæs, se arwurða   bisceop, *þone þe*   God sylf geceas
        as   Aaron   was the worthy   bishop   whom that   God self chose
        'as Aaron was, the worthy bishop, whom (that) God himself chose'
        Alc.P.XX.243, Allen (1980: 271)

The fourth possibility, often omitted in studies on relativization, is the use of a resumptive pronoun with the indeclinable particle *þe*. Traugott (1992: 230) shows that resumptive pronouns were used in all case forms. Consider:

(10)   &   þær   is mid   Estum an   mægað *þæt* <u>hi</u> (NOM)
        and there is among Ests   a   tribe   that they
        magon cyle   gewyrcan
        can   cold   make
        'and there is among the Ests a tribe who are able to freeze (the dead)'
        Or 1.21.13, Traugott (1992: 230)

(11) Se wæs Karles sunu *þe* Æþelwulf West Seaxna cyning <u>his</u> (GEN) dohtor hæfde
That was Charles' son that Æþelwulf West Saxons'king his   daughter had
him   to cuene
himself   as queen
'he was the son of Charles whose daughter was the queen of Æþelwulf,
King of the West Saxons'
Chron A (Plummer) 885.18, Traugott (1992: 206)

(12) Swa bið eac þam   treowum *þe* <u>him</u> (DAT) gecynde bið up heah   to standanne
So is   also to-those trees that to-them   natural   is up high   to stand
'so it is also with trees to which it is natural to stand up straight'
Bo 25.57.20, Traugott (1992: 229)

(13) &   ic gehwam   wille þærto tæcan *þe* <u>hiene</u> (ACC) his   lyst
ma to witanne
and I whomever shall thereto direct who him   of-it   would-please
more to know
'and I shall direct anyone to it who would like to know more about it'
Or 3 3.102.22, Traugott (1992: 229)

Traugott (1992) explains that the gap left by a relativized item is refilled by a third
person resumptive pronoun which specifies the function of the relativized NP.
Thus, resumptive pronouns appear when a relativized NP is the nominative
(subject), as in (10), the genitive (possessive relation), as in (11), the dative and
accusative (objects), as in (12) and (13), respectively. She adds that resumptive
pronouns, which occur only in *þe* relatives[4], normally follow the complementizer
immediately as evidenced by the examples above[5].

Fischer (1992: 309) echoes Traugott's observations and argues that
"resumptive pronouns seem to have a clearly defined syntactic function in both
Old and Middle English, i.e., they indicate the case of the relative particle (its
function in the subclause), which is incapable of expressing case itself. (...) *Ðe* is
in the nominative by default, but some functions such as the genitive need to be
expressed more explicitly". She adds that "resumptive pronouns should only
occur with *þe* and not with demonstrative relatives in Old English". Traugott
(1992: 229) agrees and argues that 'pronominal relativisers in OE never permit the
relativised NP position to be filled, which is what one would expect if the
pronominal relativisers are actually moved relativised NPs (in other words, one
would not expect redundancy)'. In what follows we will see that such opinions are
unwarranted.

---

4   On some rare occasions resumption is also used in *þæt* relatives (cf. Traugott 1992: 229).
5   This is not a rule, though (cf. example 11)

Other traditional studies are in the same vein. Visser (1963-1973 §75) contends that "it is well-known that instead of the later opposition *who/whose/whom* (relative pron.) the older language availed itself of the opposition *þat (þe) he/ þat his/ þat him/ þat hine* to express the same relations". Jespersen (1928: 109) rephrases the idea in the following words: "this logical analysis, which separates the connecting function (of the relative pronoun) from the case-function, has found formal expression in several languages, in which relative clauses are introduced by an invariable particle followed (sometimes at some distance) by a pronoun showing by its form or place the case relation" (Jespersen 1928: 109, MEG III, quoted in Visser 1963-1973 §604). (Visser 1963-1973 §604) notices another property of resumptive pronouns, namely their ability to disambiguate the context: "Since the OE relative particle *þe* was invariable, i.e., remained unaltered whatever its function in the syntactic unit which it introduced, utterances in which it occurred were apt to admit of more than one interpretation if context or situation were not sufficiently clear (...)".

The picture that emerges from the considerations above is that resumptive pronouns are somehow correlated with the indeclinable particle *þe* and indicate the case that this particle cannot express. Mitchell (1985 §2180-2200) offers a more detailed analysis of resumption (even though he does not use this term). He agrees that resumptive pronouns normally occur with the indeclinable particle and that they are usually found next to *þe*, indicating and/or clarifying the case relation: "the relative combination seen in OE *þe* + personal pronoun – indeclinable particle followed by pronoun showing the case relation – is not restricted to OE" (Mitchell 1985 §2198), though he extends his analysis to all three persons of personal pronouns. Contra Traugott (1992) and Fischer (1992), he also discusses resumptive pronouns in relatives other than *þe* relatives (see below). Finally, Mitchell speculates that there may be other reasons for their occurrence than the need to show the case relation, namely "stylistic, rhythmic or metrical considerations" (Mitchell 1985 §2200).

All the above analyses pose a number of problems. Firstly, the traditional studies say nothing about the apparent optionality of the resumptive strategy in Old English. In fact, relatives introduced by *þe* with the gap were much more common. Moreover, the resumptive strategy was sometimes employed when the case relation seems to be clear or, conversely, there is an absence of a resumptive pronoun where it could disambiguate the function of the relativized element. Consider examples (14) and (15):

(14) of þæm mere *þe*   Truso standeð in staðe
      of the sea which   Truso stand   on shore
      'from the sea on the shore of which Truso stands'
      coorosiu,Or_1:1.16.32.311, Pasicki (1994: 465)

(15) &   þær is mid   Estum an mægað *þæt* <u>hi</u>   magon   cyle gewyrcan
      and there is among Ests   a tribe   that they   can   cold make
      'and there is among the Ests a tribe who are able to freeze (the dead)'
      Or 1.21.13, Traugott (1992: 230), Mitchell (1985 §2195)

In (14) the relativized element is difficult to recover. In particular, the lower NP (*the sea*) that appears within the higher NP (headed by *shore*) is relativized. Thus, a resumptive pronoun (possibly preceded by a preposition) could disambiguate the context and make it easier for the language user to analyse this clause. By contrast, in (15) the resumptive pronoun could be omitted without the danger of misunderstanding.

Secondly, resumptive pronouns in oblique cases (dative and genitive) are much more common than the ones appearing in the nominative and accusative (cf. Bartnik in prep.). The quantitative difference, which is not visible in Traugott's analysis, must be somehow taken into account.

Thirdly, other types of relative clauses can also contain resumptive pronouns. For example, Mitchell (1985 §2191) notes that *se þe* relatives can be followed by a personal pronoun. This is shown in (16) below[6]:

(16) Þa wæron forðgongende   þa cristenan men 7   ða geleafsuman *þa þe*   <u>hi</u>
      then were going forth   the Christian men and the faithful   who   they
      ær...on   wudum... hi   hyddon 7 digledon
      before in woods   themselves hid   and concealed
      'Then the faithful Christians who previously hid themselves in the woods came forth'
      Bede (Ca) 42. 3, Mitchell (1985 §2191)

Examples such as (16) are unexpected if we assume the explanation that resumptives disambiguate the case relation (cf. Traugott's (1992) and Fischer's (1992) analysis).

It is not possible to deal with all the problems mentioned above in such a short article. Therefore we will focus only on one issue, namely the distribution of dative resumptive pronouns in Old English relatives. In the next section we will hypothesize that the form of the resumptive pronoun is determined by its role in the lower clause rather than by its relationship with the relative pronoun (cf. Allen 1977). What follows from this claim is that resumptive pronouns are not optional but their distribution is governed by grammatical properites of certain elements in the lower clause such as verbs and prepositions. Our hypothesis also explains the fact that dative resumptives appear both in *þe* and *se þe* relatives.

---

6   It is worth mentioning that *MS B* does not have the resumptive pronoun. This may suggest
     that we are actually looking at a *þe* relative, as shown by an alternative interpretation below:
     (i)   þa cristenan   men 7   ða geleafsuman   þa þe   <u>hi</u>
     '...   the christian   men and the faithful, those who they...'.

3. Resumptive pronouns in the dative case

Resumptive pronouns in the dative (and in the genitive) are more common than resumptives in the nominative and accusative (cf. Bartnik in prep.). This is expected because indirect objects are not easily relativized in *þe* relatives. Dative examples such as those in (17) are quite rare. However, when the dative is overtly realized, either as a relative pronoun (example 18) or as a resumptive (examples 19-20), it is regularly found. Consider:

(17) æt þam monnum... *þe*　he ða heofenlican myrhðe bodað
　　　 at the　 men　　 who 　he the heavenly　 mirth 　 proclaims
　　　 'the men to whom he proclaims the heavenly bliss'
　　　 cocathom2,ÆCHom_II,_41:307.104.6987, Mitchell (1985 §2147)

(18) æt þam Ælmihtigan Scyppende, *ðam ðe*　gehyrsumiað lif and deað
　　　 at the Almighty　 Creator　　 whom 　 obeys　　　 life and death
　　　 'the Almighty Creator to whom life and death is obedient'
　　　 cocathom1,ÆCHom_I,_31:448.244.6281, Mitchell (1985 §2192)

(19) Þa sende Galerius him ongean Seuerus mid fierde, *þe* him se onweald ær
　　　 Then sent Galerius him against Seuerus with 　 army who him the power before

　　　 geseald wæs, 7　he þær beswicen　　 wearð from his agnum monnum, 7 ofslagen
　　　 given　 was and he there betrayed　 was from his own men and killed
　　　 neah Rafenne þære byrig
　　　 near Ravenna the city
　　　 'Then Galerius sent Seuerus, to whom the power had been given earlier with an army against him, and he was betrayed there by his own men and killed near the city of Ravenna'
　　　 Or_6:30.148.11.3131

(20) & þis weorc biþ deoflum se mæsta teona; forþon þe 　 hi habbaþ manega saula on
　　　 and this work is to-devils the most annoyance because they have many souls　 in
　　　 heora gewaldum *þe* him wile git God miltsian　　 for heora mægena weorþunga
　　　 their power 　 which them will yet God show mercy for their 　 virtues' excellence
　　　 'and this work is the greatest source of annoyance to devils, because they have many souls in their power to whom God will yet show mercy on account of the excellence of their virtues'
　　　 BlHom 4. 47. 5-9

What is relativized in (19) and (20) is the indirect object of *gesellan* 'give' and *miltsian* 'have mercy on', respectively. In fact, there are many more examples with verbs that *can*[7] take and therefore relativize dative objects. These verbs include *bebeodan* 'command', *lician* 'please', *forberan* 'bear patiently', *forgifan* 'permit, forgive', *geþafian* 'allow, permit, assent to', *(ge)leanian* 'recompense', *gifan* 'give', *losian* 'be lost, perish', *ofhreowan* 'cause pity', *(ge)þafian* 'consent', and *sellan* 'give'. Since resumptive pronouns regularly appear with verbs taking dative objects they seem to participate in the argument structure of the verb rather than only clarify the case relation in *þe* relative clauses. In other words, the verbs listed above need to assign the dative case which is why they need dative resumptive pronouns, which are their overt realization.

Another argument for the important grammatical role of dative resumptive pronouns is that they are found with *se þe* relatives, which further suggests that clarifying the case relation in the relative clause is not the decisive factor. Consider the following example:

(21) Ond se bið swiðe eadig *se*   *ðe* him Drihten, se is ord   & syllend ealra
      And he is   very blessed who him Lord   who is author   and giver of-all
      eadignessa,   forgifeð,   þætte he in ðære   stowe restan   mote.
      blessedness   permits   that   he in that   place rest   can
      'and most blessed is he, to whom the Lord, who is author and giver of all
      blessedness, allows to rest in that place'
      cobede,Bede_4:31.376.23.3766

Allen (1977: 145, ft. 7), who briefly mentions resumptive (in her terminology 'returning') pronouns, observes that "an appropriate pronoun is simply inserted in the "hole" left by the moved material, and its form is determined by its role in the lower clause, rather than directly by its relationship with the relative pronoun". What is crucial for us in this short quote is the fact that she also assumes that it must be something in the lower clause (possibly the verb) that determines the form of the resumptive.

Apart from verbs, prepositions can also be accompanied by a resumptive pronoun, both in *þe* and *se þe* relatives. Consider:

(22) & mid   micle wundre, þætte se leg þurhæt   þa næglas in þæm
      and with great wonder though the fire through-consumed the nails in the
      þyrelum, þe   heo   mid þæm to þæm timbre gefæstnad wæs
      holes   which   it   with them to the timber fastened was
      'and, miraculously, though the fire broke through the nails in the holes
      wherewith it was fixed to the building'
      cobede, Bede_3:14.204.22.2081

---

7   Some of the verbs listed above can be construed with an accusative object (e.g., *forberan*).
     Then a dative object remains an option (cf. Visser 1963-73 §323, 682)

(23) Eornostlice, gif seo menifealdnys Abrahames cynnes wæs forestihtod   þurh
      Then   ift he increase Abraham's   posterity was predestined through
      Isaac, hwi underfeng he þonne unwæstmbære wif, buton   forþam þe hit is
      Isaac   how received he that   barren   wife but   because   it is
      cuð,   þæt seo forestihtung   sceolde beon mid benum gefylled, þa þa se mid
      certain that the predestination should be with prayers fulfilled when   he with
      his gebedum   beget, þæt he mihte suna habban, *se þe* on him ær   God
      his prayers   begets that he might son have   who in him before God
      forestihtode to gemenifyldenne Abrahames sæd?
      predestined to multiply   Abraham's seed
      'If, then, the increase of Abraham's posterity was predestinate by Isaac, how
      came it to pass that his wife was barren? By which most certain it is, that
      predestination is fulfilled by prayers, when as we see that he by whom God had
      predestined to increase Abraham's seed obtained by prayer to have children'
      cogregdH,GD_1_[H]:8.55.24.528

(24) Ac ðæm æfstegum is to secganne, gif hie hie   nyllað healdan wið,
      but the envious   is to be-told   if they themselves refuse to-hold against
      ðæm æfste ðæt hie weorðað besencte on ða ealdan unryhtwisnesse ðæs lytegan
      the envy   that they will-be plunged on the old   unrighteousness of-the cunning
      fiondes, *ðe* bi him   awriten is ðætte for his æfeste deað become ofer ealle eorðan.
      fiend   who by him written is that   for his envy   death came   over all earth
      'But the envious are to be told that, unless they guard against envy, they will
      be plunged into the old unrighteousness of the cunning fiend, through whose
      envy it is written that death came on the whole earth'
      cocura,CP:34.233.16.1532

Prepositions in (22), (23) and (24) require the dative case. Analogously to the
cases in (19)-(20), the appearance of the resumptives might be simply required by
the prepositions rather than by the need to clarify the case relation. It is supported
by the fact that these resumptive pronouns are used with indeclinable (examples
22, 24) and declinable (example 23) relativizers.
    There are also other structures that require the dative case. Some examples
are given below by way of illustration:

(25) Þonne þæs monnes saul ut of his lichoman gangeþ, *þe* him wæron
      when this man's soul   out of his body   goes   who him were
      ær   his æhta   leofran to hæbbenne þonne Godes   lufu
      before his possessions dearer to have   than God's   love
      'when this man's soul goes out of his body, who preferred to have his
      possessions rather than the love of God'
      coblick,HomS_14_[BlHom_4]:195.247.653

(26) Swa bið eac þam   treowum þe him gecynde bið up   heah   to standanne
      So is   also those   trees   that them natural is up   high   to stand
      'so it is also with trees to which it is natural to stand up straight'
      Bo 25.57.20, Traugott (1992: 229)

(27) Ac þa   þe him bið   unwitnode eall hiora yfel on þisseworulde habbað
      But those who them is   unpunished all their evil in this   world have
      sum yfel hefigre & frecenlicre   þonne ænig wite
      an evil   heavier and more dangerous   than any punishment
      sie   on þisse   worulde.
      should-be in this   world
      'but those whose evil is all unpunished in this world, have an evil heavier
      and more dangerous than any punishment in this world is'
      coboeth, Bo:38.119.13.2373

(28) Ond eft   he cwæð:Mara gefea   wyrð on hefonum   for anum   hreowsiendum ðonne
      and again he said   more joy   will-be in heaven   for one   repenting than
      ofer nigon & hundnigontig   ryhtwisra ðæra ðe him nan   ðearf ne bið hreowsunga.
      over nine and ninety   righteous those who them no   need not is of-repentance
      'And again, he said: There will be greater joy in heaven because of one who
      repents than over ninety-nine righteous men who need not repentance'
      cocura,CP:52.411.12.2836

(29) Ond on oðre wisan sint to manianne [...] ða   ðe   ðisse hwilendlican are
      and in other ways are to-be admonished those   who   this   transitory authority
      wilniað, & him nan gesuinc ne ðyncð ðæt hi   hie hæbben, on oðre ða ðe
      desire and it no   trouble   not think that they   it have   in other those who
      him ðyncð micel earfoðu &   micel gesuinc to habbanne, & hiera suaðeah   wilniað.
      it think   great hardship and great trouble to have   and of-it yet   desire
      'and in one way are to be admonished [...] those who desire this transitory
      authority, and think it no trouble to hold it, in another those who think it a
      great hardship and trouble to hold it, and yet desire it'
      cocura,CP:23.177.11.1186

In (25) the indirect object is probably the complement of *beon* and the
comparative of the adjective *leofran* (cf. Visser 1963-1973 §333/349). Similarly,
in (26) and (27) the adjectives *gecynde* and *unwitnode* require the dative
resumptives. As shown in (28), the indirect object can be used in the combination
of copula *beon* + indirect object + non-personal noun (cf. Visser 1963-1973
§355). Sometimes verbs other than *beon* require the dative, as shown in (29). Such
examples indicate that apart from verbs (examples (19)-(20)) and prepositions
(examples (22)-(24)) other categories, for instance adjectives can subcategorize

resumptives. This fact further supports the hypothesis that it is the lower clause rather than the relationship with the relative pronoun that determines the role and function of resumptive pronouns. Needless to say that in such cases as those presented above the relativizer does not have to be indeclinable.

There are also more problematic cases. Consider the following examples:

(30) Eala, hwæt ðæt bið gesælig mon *þe* him ealne weg ne hangað nacod
     O   how that is happy man who him all   way not hangs   naked
     sweord ofer ðæm heafde be smale þræde, swa swa me git symle dyde?
     sword over the head   by small thread just as me yet   ever done
     'O, how happy is the man, over whose head a naked sword does not always
     hang on a thin thread, as it has ever yet done to me!'
     coboeth,Bo:29.65.27.1226

(31) & him eac gesægð hu ðæm monnum *ðe* him   mægen & cræft   wiexð, hu him
     and him also tells how the man   who him virtue and wisdom grows how him
     eac hwilum   eakiað   æfter ðæm   mægenum ða costunga
     also often   increase   after the   excellence the temptations
     'and tells him how, when a man's virtue and wisdom increase, his
     temptations also often increase in proportion to his excellence'
     cocura,CP:21.163.5.1107

In examples (30)-(31) the situation is slightly different: the dative resumptives appear even though the verbs *weaxan* 'grow' and *hangian* 'hang' do not require indirect objects. This means that the resumptives are not required by the argument structure of the verbs. Note, however, that both examples have a strong affinity with the genitive constructions, as shown in the translations of these sentences. Recall that Old English did not have a genitive relativizer (in Modern English we have *whose*), which often necessitated the use of a resumptive pronoun to indicate the possessive relation. This close relation between the dative and the genitive in examples (30)-(31) might account for the use of the dative resumptives in these structures (cf. Fischer 1992: 309, Bartnik in prep.)

4. Conclusions

The relatively large number of sentences with dative resumptives indicate that they deserve a thorough study. Cursory descriptions in the standard books cannot do justice to this aspect of grammar and appear to contain unwarranted generalizations. First, even if resumptives clarify case relations between the main and subordinate clause it cannot be their main function. Resumptives appear in Old English because they perform very important grammatical functions and their form is determined by their role in the lower clause rather than by their relationship with the relative pronoun (cf. Allen 1977). In other words, they seem to be required by grammatical properties of verbs, prepositions or other elements such as the verb *beon* and the comparative of the adjective *leofran*. This is also supported by the fact that dative resumptives appear both in *þe* and *se þe* relatives. Finally, resumptive relatives seem to complement each other with gapped relatives, i.e., without resumptive pronouns. This is another argument for the controlled rather than optional and random use of these structures (cf. Bartnik in prep.).

References

Allen, Cynthia L.
    1977   Topics in diachronic syntax. [Unpublished Ph.D. dissertation, University
                of Massachusetts.]
    1980   "Movement and deletion in Old English", *Linguistic Inquiry* 11: 261-324.
Bartnik, Artur
    [in prep.] "The distribution of resumptive pronouns in Old English".
Blake, Norman (ed.)
    1992   *The Cambridge history of the English language*. Vol. II. Cambridge:
                Cambridge University Press.
Bondaruk, Anna
    1995   "Resumptive pronouns in English and Polish", in: Edmund Gussmann
                (ed.), 27-55.
Bosworth, Joseph – T. Northcote Toller
    1898   *An Anglo-Saxon dictionary based on the manuscript collections of the
                late Joseph Bosworth* (available at: http://lexicon.ff.cuni.cz/texts/
                oe_bosworthtoller_about.html)
DOE = *Dictionary of Old English in electronic form* (letters A-F) – available at:
                http://www.doe.utoronto.ca
Everaert, Martin – Henk van Riemsdijk (eds.)
    2006   *The Blackwell companion to syntax*. Vol. VI. Oxford: Blackwell.
Fischer, Olga
    1992   "Syntax", in: Norman Blake (ed.), 207-408.
Gibińska, Marta – Zygmunt Mazur (eds.)
    1994   *Literature and language in the intertextual and intercultural context.*
                Kraków: Uniwersytet Jagielloński.
Gussmann, Edmund (ed.)
    1995   *Licensing in syntax and phonology*. Lublin: Folium.
Hogg, Richard (ed.)
    1992   *The Cambridge history of the English language*. Vol. I. Cambridge:
                Cambridge University Press.

Jespersen, Otto
    1928   *A modern English grammar on historical principles*. London: Allen and Unwin.
Keenan, Edward – Bernard Comrie
    1977   "Noun phrase accessibility and universal grammar", *Linguistic Inquiry* 8: 63-99.
McCloskey, James
    2006   "Resumption", in: Martin Everaert – Henk van Riemsdijk (eds.), 94-117.
McKee, Cecile – Dana McDaniel
    2001   "Resumptive pronouns in English relative clauses", *Language Acquisition* 9(2): 113-156.
Mitchell, Bruce
    1985   *Old English syntax*. 2 Vols. Oxford: Clarendon Press.
Pasicki, Adam
    1994   "Old English relatives: How to recover case?", in: Marta Gibińska – Zygmunt Mazur (eds.), 451-473.
Sells, Peter
    1984   *Syntax and semantics of resumptive pronouns*. [Unpublished Ph.D. dissertation. University of Massachusetts.]
Taylor, Ann – Anthony Warner – Susan Pintzuk – Frank Beths
    2003   *The York-Toronto-Helsinki Parsed Corpus of Old English Prose*. York: University of York.
Traugott, Elizabeth
    1992   "Syntax", in: Richard Hogg (ed.), 168-289.
Visser, Fredericus T.
    1963-1973   *An historical syntax of the English language.* 4 Vols. Leiden: EJ Brill.

Toward a diachronic account of English prepositional subordinators expressing purpose: *To the intent that*

Jerzy Nykiel, University of Silesia
Andrzej M. Łęcki, Pedagogical University of Cracow

ABSTRACT

The main focus of this article falls on the adverbial subordinator of purpose *to the intent that*, which develops in the early fourteenth century and persists till the early eighteenth century. The rationale behind this research stems from the need to systematically account for the emergence, use, and decline of English purpose subordinators other than *(so) that*. Kortmann's (1997) remark that Middle English contributes the greatest number of adverbial subordinators in the history of English helps accommodate the timeframe of the emergence of *to the intent that*. Further, data are presented indicating that the predecessor of *to the intent that* is, most likely, Anglo-Norman *a l'entente que* which predates the first attestations of the English subordinator. With the aid of grammaticalization theory, stages are shown through which the noun *intent*, through the use in prepositional phrases, becomes part of a purpose subordinator. With the grammaticalization of *to the intent that* running its course by 1500, the focus is shifted to the process of subjectification. The development of *to the intent that* turns out to reflect subjectification as construed from two different points of view, namely Traugott's (1995, 2010) and Langacker's (1990).

1. Introduction

Despite a recent surge in research interest in the diachrony of English adverbial subordinators, purpose clauses reside far from the spotlight. A case in point would be the contributions in Lenker and Meurman-Solin (2007), a volume devoted to English connectives, in which no note is taken of purpose subordinators, purpose clauses being only discussed briefly in connection with infinitival *to* by Los (2007). It seems that often purpose subordinators or purpose functions of subordinators are only mentioned in passing or as margin notes while other issues are discussed, e.g., Molencki's (2008: 212) remark about the brief use of *because* as a purpose subordinator in Middle English in a study revolving around the causal function of *because*.

Part of the reason why purpose subordinators do not attract much attention is that a prototypical finite purpose clause in English has been introduced by *(so)* *that* ever since the Old English times. When Schmidtke-Bode (2009: 30) speaks about the purpose construction in Present-day English, she illustrates it with a sentence containing purposive *so that*:

(1) *We went to the concert early <u>so that</u> we would get good seats.*

An adverbial clause of purpose, besides being introduced by a subordinator, has a main verb either preceded by a modal verb or taking subjunctive marking in early

English, "[a]s the event described by this clause has not yet come to pass at the time of utterance" (Los 2007: 37). It does seem, however, that a diachronic account of purpose subordinators other than (*so*) *that* and of their grammaticalization is missing. In this paper we seek to fill the void and address the issue of the rise, development and decline of *to the intent that,* a subordinator introducing finite clauses of purpose beginning with the fourteenth century. Our discussion begins with Middle English as this is when a number of prepositional purpose subordinators such as *to the intent that, to the end that* and *to the effect that* (see Łęcki and Nykiel 2011 for the latter two) surface. Offering insights into Old English data, Shearin (1903) and Mitchell (1985) show that prepositional subordinators exist already in Old English, yet the dominant trend at this point is for a preposition to take a pronominal complement while nominal complements are, as Shearin (1903: 63) argues, exceptional.

The remaining part of this study is divided into three sections. Section 2 explores the assimilation of the French loanword *intent* in Middle English and shows its gravitation toward grammaticalized uses. Section 3 explicitly tackles the grammaticalization of *to the intent that* into a subordinator while Section 4 shows how the process of subjectification bears upon the development of the subordinator. The following corpora have been made use of to compile data for this study: the *Middle English Dictionary* (henceforth *MED*) corpus, the *Dictionnaire du Moyen Français* (henceforth *DMF*) corpus, the *Helsinki Corpus* (henceforth *HC*), the *Corpus of Early English Correspondence* (henceforth *CEEC*), *ARCHER*, and the *Lampeter Corpus*.

2. Origins and a French connection

Kortmann (1997: 299) includes *to the intent that* among adverbial subordinators innovated in Middle English, yet he does not comment on the origin of the form. The noun *entente/intent* appears in English in the early thirteenth century denoting "purpose or intention; aim or object; reason (for doing something)" (cf. *MED* s.v. *entente* def.1.). The noun is a Middle French loanword and, according to *CEDEL* s.v. *intent*, it arose as a participial substantive of the verb *entendre* 'to intend', which goes back to Latin *intendere* 'bend or apply the mind to'. The utmost Indo-European roots of *intendere* are to be sought in PIE *ten-* 'to stretch' (cf. *AHDIER* s.v. *ten-*). The earliest instances of the ME *intent* come from *Ancrene Riwle* and are shown in examples (2) and (3):

(2)   *Haue in al þet tu dest an of þes twa **ententes.***
      'Have in all that thou doest one of these two intents.'
                                   c1230(?a1200) *Ancr.*(Corp-C 402) 104b

(3)   *Ant tah min entente beo to beten ham her inne, ich hit do se poureliche.*
'And though my intent is to atone for them in this, I do it so poorly.'
c1230(?a1200) **Ancr.*(Corp-C 402) 16b

Beginning with the fourteenth century, instances of *intent* appear in abundance, the sense of purpose being visible especially in prepositional phrases:

(4)   *Ne in non oper entente we hider ne come.*
'We came hither with no other purpose/intention.'
c1325(c1300) *Glo.Chron.A* (Clg A.11) 10358

(5)   *And in such place as pought hem auanntage For here entent pey tooke her herburgage.*
'And in a place which seemed to them advantageous for their purpose they took their lodging'
(c1390) Chaucer *CT.ML.*(Manly-Rickert) B.147

(6)   *For sythyn that I only am sent to this entent, I be myn one schal bothe the sqwete and the soure For yow endure;*
'Since I am only sent for this purpose, I shall myself endure the good and the bad for you;'
(1449) Metham *AC* (Gar 141) 1412

At the same time *intent*, when preceded by a preposition, introduces infinitival clauses:

(7)   *Now wole I speke of lesynges whiche gener|ally is fals signifiaunce of worde in entente to desceyuen his euen cristene.*
'Now I want to speak about falsehood which is generally a false meaning of a word with a view to deceiving a fellow Christian.'
(c1390) Chaucer *CT.Pars.*(Manly-Rickert) I 608

(8)   *Achilles..Lep vp full lyuely..To pat entent..To deire Ector with dethe.*
'Achilles leapt up vigorously in order to kill Hector.'
c1540(?a1400) *Destr.Troy* (Htrn 388) 8647

(9)   *Whan pou dost ony good dede for pat ende & for pat entent, princypally, to be preysed perfore.*
'When you do something good in order to be, above all, praised for that.'
c1450 Jacob's W.(Sal 174) 71/18

(10) *And he dude **in thilke entent** to be afore, and haue awey the dameselle.*
      'And he did in order to be ahead and keep the young woman at a distance.'
                                   a1500(?1450) *GRom.*(Hrl 7333) 38,39

To the intent that emerges as an adverbial subordinator well into the latter part of
the fourteenth century. We have identified the first instances in the works of
Gower and Chaucer after running a check on the *MED* corpus. The corpora of
later English (the EME part of the *HC*, *CEEC*, *ARCHER*, *Lampeter*) point to the
early eighteenth century as the time when the subordinator fades away. The use of
to the intent that may have been inspired or reinforced by the parallel function of
Anglo-Norman *a l'entente que*, which in the *Anglo-Norman Dictionary*, s.v.
entente, is rendered as 'with the intention that, to the end that'. Relevant examples
follow below, (11) indicating that the subordinator use of the construction has a
longer pedigree in Anglo-Norman than in English:

(11) *Lui Emperour orgoillous, qe vist la disconfiture de ses gentz, s'en fuist^{V1}*
      erraument et la nuyt ensuant se herbergea a cynk lieux^{V2} d'illoeqes ove touz
      *ses gentz fuantz, **a l'entente q'il** purroit relier ses gentz ove l'eide des gentz*
      du paiis environ.
      The proud emperor, who saw the defeat of his people, departed immediately
      and, the night approaching, found lodging five miles away from there along
      with all his fleeing people so that he could reassemble his people with the
      aid of the local around."
                                              c.1250 *Rich* 1 25.24

(12) *alent[ent] (l. a l'entent) qe [...] loure lessoures, lours heires ne lour*
      assignés ne ducent avoir conusaunce dez loures nounes
      "so that their lessors, their heirs and their agents will not have to know their
      names"
                                                        Stats ii 280

(13) *diverses ordeignances sont faitz [...] **al entent qe** bon drap et loial seroit*
      faitz en la ville
      "various ordinances are passed so that cloth of good quality will be made in
      this town"
                                                        Bristol ii 40

Interestingly, it seems that the purpose subordinator *a l'entente que* never
becomes even a temporary fixture in mediaeval continental French. *A l'entente
que* does not show up in the *DMF* corpus, which contains Middle French texts of
the 1330-1500 period, nor is it mentioned by *DMF*, a dictionary of mediaeval
French. If *to the intent that* is then a calque rather than an English development, it
is modeled on Anglo-Norman *a l'entente que*. A similar plot of the action has

been observed before by, for instance, Molencki (2008: 205ff.), who argues that the use of English *because* in the fourteenth century is preceded by earlier attestations of Anglo-Norman *a/par cause que* rather than by those of any French form.

3. Grammaticalization of *to the intent that*

A grammaticalized use of the lexical string *to the intent that* has this structure cast into the role of an adverbial subordinator introducing finite purpose clauses. As noted in the previous section, this process begins in the late fourteenth century, an index to there being almost a two hundred year gap between the first appearance of *intent* in English and the onset of grammaticalization. Our aim in this section is to take stock of the steps that *to the intent that* takes on the road to becoming a purpose subordinator.

At first, the form of the subordinator allows significant variety in that the preposition introducing the subordinator can also be *in, for,* or *till,* as in examples (14) through (16):

(14) *And þan with grete reuerence he takez of þe dung and rubbez it on his visage and his breste, as he did with þe vryn, **in þat entent þat** he be fulfilled with þe vertu of þe haly ox and þat he be blissed with þat haly thing.*
   'And then with great reverence he (the king) takes some of the excrement and rubs it on his face and breast, as he did with the urine, so that he will be filled with the virtue of the holy ox and blessed with that holy thing.'
   ?a1452 *Mandev.(2)* (Eg 1982)

(15) *And the thirde, þat seid, "sothely I slow him with myn owne hondys," þat is euery synner, þat owiþ to graunte þe sothe in confession, **for the entente þat** the Innocent soule sholde not be slayne; & þenne yf he do so, withe oute dowte he shal not dye, but he shalle have euerlastyng lyfe.*
   'And the third said, "Truly I killed him with my own hands," that is to say, every sinner ought to tell the truth at the confession, so that the innocent soul should not be killed; and if he does that, certainly he shall not die but he shall have everlasting life.'
   a1500(?1450) *GRom.*(Hrl 7333) 205

(16) *Þe seuent was of Clay, **till þat entent þat** a man þat es raysed vp to þe dingnyte of a kyng sulde alway vmbythynk hym þat he was made of erthe,*
   'The seventh was made of clay so that a man who is raised to the dignity of the king should always remember that he is made of earth,'
   c1440 PL*Alex.*(Thrn) 57/33

As can be seen in the previous examples, the noun *intent* usually requires a determiner, the demonstrative pronouns *thilke/this/that* and the article *the* alternating in the determiner position. Optionally *intent* can be modified by *swich/such*:

(17) *Ye shul first in alle youre werkes mekely biseken to the heighe god þat he wol be youre conseillour. And shapeth yow **to swich entente that** he yeue yow conseil and confort ...*
      'You should first of all in all your work meekly beseech mighty god to be your advisor and shape you so that you can have his advice and comfort...'
                              (c1390) Chaucer *CT.Mel.*(Manly-Rickert) B.2306

(18) *In Egypt also þere ben dyuerse langages & dyuerse lettres ... I schall deuyse ȝou suche as þei ben And the names how thei clepen hem, **To such entent þat** ȝee mowe knowe the difference of hem & of othere.*
      'In Egypt there are various languages and alphabets ... I shall describe them for you as they are used and the words by which they call them so that you can know the difference between those and others.'
                              ?a1425(c1400) *Mandev.(1)* (Tit C.16) 34/24

Quite frequently the ME phrase *the entente* as part of the purposive subordinator *to the entente that* is paired with another synonymous phrase such as *the ende* or *the effecte*, most probably for reasons of emphasis, as in the following examples:

(19) *Right so he þat was formyour of all the world wolde suffre for vs at ierusalem þat is the myddes of the world **to þat ende & entent þat** his passioun & his deth þat was pupplischt þere myghte ben knowen euenly to all the parties of the world.*
      'Rightly so, he that was the creator of the world wanted to suffer for us in Jerusalem, which is the center of the world, so that his passion and death, which were revealed there, could be made known to all the parts of the world.'
                              a1425(c1400) *Mandev.(1)* (Tit C.16) 2/8

(20) *Wherfore I pray yow lat mercy been in youre mynde and in youre herte **to theffect and entente þat** god almyghty haue mercy on yow in his laste Iuggement;*
      'Wherefore I beg you, let mercy be in your mind and heart so that almighty God will have mercy on you in his last judgment;'
                              (c1390) Chaucer *CT.Mel.*(Manly-Rickert) B.3058

The choice of these two phrases is far from accidental as *to the ende that* and *to the effecte that* also grammaticalize into purpose subordinators in Middle English, as shown by Łęcki and Nykiel (2011)

It is significant to note that no such variation is possible after the year 1500. The end of the ME period seems a watershed in the grammaticalization of *to the intent that* in that from that point onward the shape of the subordinator is fixed. The only alterations occasionally admitted are cliticization of the determiner upon *intent*, as in (21) and (22):

(21) *Furst the said Duke deasired thre monthes licence of the King and Lordes **to th'intent** in that tyme he mought departe in France and retorne in Scotland again for certain considerations moving the King and Wele of Scotland,*
                          1524 CEECS\ LETTER LXXXV 242

(22) *Pisistratus in Athens, who launched himself **to th'intent that** by the sighte of bleedinge woundes, the people might beleve he was set vppon:*
                          1570-1640 \helsinki\eme\cetri2a 14

and loss of the complementizer *that,* which is also illustrated in example (21) above. It needs to be said, however, that both inclinations are continuations of ME patterns rather than EModE innovations (see, for example, Rissanen (1997) for the issue of co-occurrence of the complementizer *that* with ME adverbial subordinators).

No reliable account of the line of development of *to the intent that* proposed above can be made without embracing grammaticalization theory. Studies of grammaticalization such as Hopper (1991), Hopper and Traugott (1993: 113ff.), and Lehmann (2002) have paid attention to a number of parameters that go side by side with and are indicative of gramamticalization. Two of those parameters, namely obligatorification and decategorialization, merit singling out in the case of *to the intent that*. Obligatorification is characterized by Lehmann (2002: 124) as "the reduction of transparadigmatic variability". This, in other words, means that a construction which initially allowed any (or none) of a group of items in a paradigm to fill a given slot in this construction, now obligatorily requires selection of only one of those items. Obligatorification of *to the intent that* can be seen in the initial freedom of choice when it comes to the preposition, in which case the choice is between *to, in, for* and *till,* and to the determiner, the range of which covers *thilke, this, that* and *the*. The freedom ends when one form in each set, that is the preposition *to* and the determiner *the,* comes to be treated as obligatory. The loss of the modification and conjunction options which visits *the intent* as part of the subordinator can be explained via decategorialization, another feature put forward in the context of grammaticalization. Decategorialization is understood by Hopper (1991: 22), Hopper and Traugott (1993: 103ff.) and

Brinton and Traugott (2005: 25ff.) as a drift away from membership or prototypical membership in a given category and loss of features typical of that category. No longer an ordinary determiner phrase, *the intent* now has an appendage role as part of the make-up of the grammaticalized subordinator *to the intent that*.

The grammaticalization of *to the intent that* seems nearly complete when the subordinator is used on a par with purposive *(so) that*. This is clearly visible in ME examples where a matrix clause is followed by two clauses of purpose. The first clause is introduced by *(so) that* while the other takes *to the intent that*, which has its illustration in examples (23) and (24):

(23) *Or ell men coueren the pytt with with grauell & sond, þat noman schall*
      perceyue where ne knowe where the pytt is, to þat entent þat neuer after
      none of his frendes schull han mynde ne remembrance of him.
      'Or else men cover the pit with gravel or sand so that no one will notice or
      know where the pit is, so that none of his friends will ever remember him.'
                            ?a1425(c1400) *Mandev.(1)* (Tit C.16) 168/4

(24) *Thenne Kyng Marke bethoughte hym that he wold haue syre Tristram vnto*
      that turnement desguysed that no man shold knowe hym to that entente that
      the haute prynce shold wene that sir Tristram were syre launcelot
      'Then Kink Mark decided that he would have sir Tristram disguised at the
      tournament so that no one should recognize him, so that the high prince
      should believe that sir Tristram was sir Lancelot'
                                  (a1470) Malory *Wks.*(Win-C) 494/3

Concurrently, this co-occurrence of an older purpose marker and a newly grammaticalized one is a case of layering, that is a situation in which a more established grammatical form exists alongside a form grammaticalized later (see Hopper 1991: 22).

To the intent that persists till the early eighteenth century, although it should be said that in the eighteenth century there are only two instances culled from a 1724 political text entitled "An examination and resolution of the two questions following, (…)" found in the *Lampeter Corpus*. It seems safe to assume that in the early eighteenth century *to the intent that* survives only in officialese only to be ousted from English soon thereafter. The function of the purpose subordinator is taken over by newly grammaticalizing forms such as *in order that* (cf. Łęcki and Nykiel forthcoming).

It can be concluded that a grammaticaliztion process observed with regards to *to the intent that* becomes transparent in view of Rissanen's (2007: 194)) scenario delineating a common pattern whereby ME adverbial subordinators emerge. The pattern builds on an early ME loan-word which, through the use in prepositional phrases, expands into a subordinator in the fourteenth century. *To the intent that* subscribes to this pattern to the extent that its grammaticalization begins in the fourteenth century, i.e., almost two centuries after English accommodates the lexical item *intent*. Once the process is set in motion, however, it progresses quickly in that barely a few decades intervene between the first occurrences of *to the intent that* and its quite advanced grammaticalization. This in turn suggests that after all the initial spark that triggers the grammatical function of *to the intent that* comes from Anglo-Norman *a l'entente que*. In the next section we seek to find whether the gramaticalization of *to the intent that* intersects with subjectification.

4. Toward increasing subjectivity

The aim of the following discussion is to assess to what extent, if at all, *to the intent that* in the course of the grammatical development detailed in section 3 becomes subject to subjectification. A motivation for this type of research arises from Traugott's (2010: 390f.) claim that grammaticalization and subjectification tend to co-occur. Among various approaches to subjectification and subjectivity, it is Traugott's (2010) that has primarily diachronic relevance. Traugott (1995: 48, 2010: 34) and Traugott and Dasher (2005: 225) talk about a cline of subjectification which indicates that in the course of time non- or less subjective expressions tend to become more subjective, that is "recruited by the speaker to encode and regulate attitudes and beliefs" (Traugott 2010: 35). Subsequently, some subjective forms have been attested to develop addressee-oriented functions, which is handled under the notion of intersubjectification on the cline. If intersubjectification does not apply to *to the intent that*, the subjectification (and gramaticalization) of this structure begins when the form comes to be used to express a discourse participant's intention. By default, a desiderative predicate surfaces in the matrix clause followed by the clause introduced by *to the intent that*. Since *to the intent that* serves to expand on one's intention, it is unlikely that we can talk about any initial objectivity at the beginning of the subjectification process. Still, subjectivity seems weakest when the speaker mentions his or her own intention, as in

(25)   *Yet wol I it expresse **To thentente that** men may be war ther by.*
    'Yet I want to say it so that men may thereby become aware.'
                     (c1395) Chaucer CT.CY.(Manly-Rickert) G.1306

When the speaker and the person expressing an intention are separate, we have to do with increased subjectivity as "[a] speaker does not have access to the addressee's mind" (Traugott and Dasher 2005: 91) and thus can only speculate about it. A case in point would be, for example, (19):

(19) *Right so he þat was formyour of all the world wolde suffre for vs at ierusalem þat is the myddes of the world to þat ende & entent þat his passioun & his deth þat was pupplischt þere myghte ben knowen euenly to all the parties of the world.*

'Rightly so, he that was the creator of the world wanted to suffer for us in Jerusalem, which is the center of the world, so that his passion and death, which were revealed there, could be made known to all the parts of the world.'

a1425(c1400) *Mandev.(1)* (Tit C.16) 2/8

As the content of the intention is laid out in the finite clause following *to the intent that*, either marked for the subjunctive mood or containing a modal verb, the *to the intent that* clause must be treated as an adverbial clause. Such a clause invites an inference of purpose as an intended state of affairs may be conceived as a goal which the matrix clause participant wishes to obtain. The inference is generalized when the matrix clause no longer contains a desiderative predicate and *to the intent that* can be interpreted as a subordinator of purpose. Even when it happens, however, the participant's intention to bring about the desired state of affairs remains somewhat present. Cristofaro (2003: 57ff.) argues that the participant's will to bring the proposition expressed in the adverbial clause to fruition is inherent to purpose relations. This, on the other hand, ties in with the fact observed by Schmidtke-Bode (2009), that the development of purposive subordinators from desiderative expressions is common cross-linguistically.

Now that *to the intent that* is a subordinator, it grows more subjective in that it enables speakers to affirm purpose relations, in other words, it develops a textual function as Traugott (1995, 2010) sees it. Witness examples (16) above, (26), and (27) which are devoid of any desiderative predicate in the matrix clause:

(26) *Thre of the grettest shippes of Scotland er left in Fraunce to the spryng of the yere, **to th'entent** thei may assist the French navye as it is supposed.*

1513 CEECS\LETTER XXXIV 98

(27) *In like maner the Image of the Crucifixx is hunge vp in euery Church, **to the entent that** we may see how greeuouslie sinne was punyshed in that most blessed bodye of our Sauyour Christ Iesu,*

1500-1570 helsinki\eme\ceserm1a 69

Note also that these examples do not make explicit (or do not profile) the participant interested in realizing the proposition in the purpose clause. As a result, the point of reference, that is to say, the intent to bring about the state of affairs rests with the speaker. This seems crucial to Langacker's (1990) take on subjectivity, itself quite removed from Traugott's (1995, 2010). The key to increased subjectivity in this approach would be the fact that the situation, in absence of any participant that could be held accountable for the expression of the intention and/or purpose, is interpreted as the speaker's point of view. Since the more subjective sentences such as (16), (26) and (27) can be found for the first time in the fifteenth century and continue in the sixteenth century, that is later than the objective examples, e.g., (25), they help make a case for Langacker's (1990) diachronic subjectification.

5. Conclusion

This paper has been taken up with unraveling the history of *to the intent that*, a purpose subordinator innovated in Middle English and lost in the eighteenth century. The development of the subordinator should be seen as proceeding along the INTENTION-to-PURPOSE path, the intention component being secured by the early thirteenth century loanword noun *entent*. It takes roughly two centuries for grammaticalization to begin in the late fourteenth century. It seems the chief reasons why *to the intent that* undergoes grammaticalization in the first place are the availability of the meaning of purpose when the noun occurs in prepositional phrases and the fact that in the Anglo-Norman dialect a subordinator of purpose involving the same noun is already in use. The data gathered suggest a fairly abrupt character of the grammaticalization process, given that grammaticalized instances, in which *to the intent that* functions as an alternative to the firmly established purpose subordinator (*so*) *that*, crop up as early as in the first half of the fifteenth century. Such quick grammaticalization can be ascribed to *to the intent that* being a copy of the Anglo-Norman pattern.

We have shown how obligatorification and decategorialization impinge upon the grammaticalization of *to the intent that* in Middle English, leaving no room for any grammatical developments after that period. On top of that, the grammaticalization has been found, quite unsurprisingly, to run parallel to subjectification, in the course of which *to the intent that* segues from a less subjective to a more subjective use. While in the former it merely serves to convey the discourse participant's intention, in the latter it helps express a purpose relation construed from the speaker's point of view.

Dictionaries

AHDIER = Calvert Watkins (ed.), 2000. *The American Heritage Dictionary of Indo-European Roots*. Boston-New York: Houghton Mifflin.
CEDEL = Walter W. Skeat (ed.), 1965. *A Concise Etymological Dictionary of the English Language*. Oxford: The Clarendon Press.
DMF = *le Dictionnaire du Moyen Français online* available at: http://www.cnrtl.fr/definition/dmf/
MED = *Middle English Dictionary online* available at: http://ets.umdl.umich.edu/m/mec
The Anglo-Norman Dictionary online available at: http://www.anglo-norman.net

References

Amano, Masachiyo – Michiko Ogura – Masayuki Ohkado (eds.)
2008   *Historical Englishes in varieties of texts and contexts*. Frankfurt am Mein: Peter Lang.
Brinton, Laurel J. – Elizabeth C. Traugott
2005   *Lexicalization and language change*. Cambridge: Cambridge University Press.
Cristofaro, Sonia
2003   *Subordination*. Oxford: Oxford University Press.
Davidse, Kristin – Lieven Vandelanotte – Hubert Cuyckens (eds.)
2010   *Subjectification, intersubjectification and grammaticalization.* Berlin – New York: Walter de Gruyter.
Heine, Bernd – Tania Kuteva
2002   *World lexicon of grammaticalization*. Cambridge: Cambridge University Press.
Hickey, Raymond – Stanisław Puppel (eds.)
1997   *Language history and linguistic modelling: A festschrift for Jacek Fisiak on his 60ᵗʰ birthday*. Berlin: Mouton de Gruyter.
Hopper, Paul J.
1991   "On some principles of grammaticalization', in: Elizabeth Closs Traugott – Bernd Heine (eds.), 17-35.
Hopper, Paul J. – Elizabeth Closs Traugott
1993   *Grammaticalization*. Cambridge: Cambridge University Press.
Kortmann, Bernd
1997   *Adverbial subordination: A typology and history of adverbial subordinators based on European languages*. Berlin-New York: Mouton de Gruyter.

Langacker, Ronald W.
1990   "Subjectification", *Cognitive Linguistics* 1-1: 5-38.

Lehmann, Christian
2002   *Thoughts on grammaticalization.* Erfurt: ASSidUE 9.
Lenker, Ursula – Anneli Meurman-Solin (eds.)
2007   *Connectives in the history of English.* Amsterdam – Philadelphia: John Benjamins.
Los, Bettelou
2007   "To as a connective in the history of English", in: Ursula Lenker – Anneli Meurman-Solin (eds.), 31-60.
Łęcki, Andrzej M. – Jerzy Nykiel
2011   "All roads lead to PURPOSE: The rise of *to the end that* and *to the effect that* in early English", paper presented at the Seventh International Conference on Middle English (ICOME 7), Lviv, 3-5 August 2011.
[forthcoming] "Grammaticalisation of the English prepositional conjunction *in order to/that*"
Mitchell, Bruce
1985   *Old English syntax.* Vol. I and II. Oxford: Clarendon Press.
Molencki, Rafał
2008   "The rise of *because* in Middle English", in: Masachiyo Amano – Michiko Ogura – Masayuki Ohkado (eds.), 201-215.

Rissanen, Matti
1997   "Optional THAT with subordination in Middle English", in: Raymond Hickey – Stanisław Puppel (eds.), 373-383.
2007   "The development of adverbial subordinators in early English"' in: Matti Rissanen – Marianna Hintikka – Leena Kahlas-Tarkka – Rod McConchie (eds.), 173-210.
Rissanen, Matti – Marianna Hintikka – Leena Kahlas-Tarkka – Rod McConchie (eds.),
2007   *Change in meaning and the meaning of change: Studies in semantics and grammar from Old to Present-Day English.* Helsinki: Société Néophilologique.
Schmidtke-Bode, Karsten
2009   *A Typology of purpose clauses.* Amsterdam – Philadelphia: John Benjamins.
Shearin, Hubert G.
1903   *The expression of purpose in Old English prose.* New York: Henry Holt and Company.
Stein, Dieter – Susan Wright (eds.).
1995   *Subjectivity and subjectivisation.* Cambridge: Cambridge University Press.
Traugott, Elizabeth Closs
1995   "Subjectification in grammaticalization", in: Dieter Stein – Susan Wrigh (eds.), 31-54.

2010   "(Inter)subjectivity and (inter)subjectification: A reassessment", in:
              Kristin Davidse – Lieven Vandelanotte – Hubert Cuyckens (eds.), 29-71.
Traugott, Elizabeth Closs – Richard B. Dasher
      2005   *Regularity in semantic change.* Cambridge: Cambridge University Press.
Traugott, Elizabeth Closs – Bernd Heine (eds.)
      1991   *Approaches to gramaticalization.* Amsterdam – Philadelphia: John
              Benjamins.

The semantic field TASTE in Old and Middle English[1]

Magdalena Bator, Academy of Management, Warsaw

ABSTRACT

Since the Old English times the semantic field TASTE has undergone a number of changes, as a result of which it became almost completely restructured. Of the words belonging to the field in Old English, only *smæc* seems to have remained within the field until the Present Day English. All the other Old English words disappeared from the language, and their place was taken by new lexemes, mostly borrowed from French, introduced into English in the Middle English period.

The word which dominated the field, *taste*, had been first recorded in the 13th c. Originally, it referred to the sense of touch. Only in the second half of the 14th c. did *taste* undergo a shift of meaning and appeared with the sense 'the act of tasting, or perceiving by flavour of a thing with the organ of taste' (*OED*).

The present paper analyses the semantic field TASTE in the Old and Middle English periods. Occasionally, references will be made to Early Modern English.

1. Introduction

The present paper concentrates on the analysis of the lexical items belonging to the semantic field TASTE. The study has been restricted to nouns denoting 'taste' in its general sense. The data for the present study have been collected from a number of dictionaries: *The Oxford English Dictionary* (*OED*), *the Middle English Dictionary* (*MED*), Bosworth and Toller's *Anglo-Saxon Dictionary* (*ASD*), *Thesaurus of Old English* (*TOE*) and *the Historical Thesaurus of English* (*HTE*); as well as from a number of textual corpora: *the Helsinki Corpus* (*HC*), *the Toronto Corpus* (*TC*), *the Innsbruck Corpus of Middle English Prose* (*IC*), and *the Lampeter Corpus* (*LC*).

Following the two thesauri, the Old English semantic field TASTE comprised such lexical items as: *swæc, smæc, hunigsmæc, sealt,* and a number of derivatives of the noun (*ge*)*birg* 'taste', e.g., *abirging, onbyrignes, gebirg, gebirging* and *birgnes*. Only *smæc* and *swæc* made their way into the Middle English period, however, with some changes within their referential field. In Middle English the semantic field was enriched with such nouns as *savour, sapor, relese (relish), tarage* and *taste*, majority of which were borrowed from French.

---

1   The publication of the present paper has been made possible with the financial support of the Foundation for Polish Science.

A number of nouns both in Old and Middle English shared their referential field with another sense, i.e., 'smell', e.g., *smæc, swæc, reles, taste, savour* and *tang*, and, in the case of the word *taste*, also with the sense of 'touch'.

2. TASTE

2.1 OE *smæc*, ME *smack, smatch*

Smæc (PDE *smack*) was first recorded in 1000. According to the *OED*, in the Old English period it was used with the senses: (i) 'a taste or flavour; the distinctive or peculiar taste of sth, or a special flavour distinguishable from this' and (ii) 'scent, odour, smell'. In the Middle English period some additional senses were recorded: (iii) 'the sense or faculty of taste' (obs.) and (iv) 'delight or enjoyment; inclination, relish' (obs.). In Early Modern English, on the one hand, sense (ii) became obsolete, and thus, the association of *smæc* with the semantic field SMELL disappeared. On the other, a number of new senses were added: (v) 'pleasant or agreeable taste or relish' (obs.), (vi) 'a trace, tinge, or suggestion of sth specified', (vii) 'a slight or superficial knowledge; a smattering' (obs. in 18th c.), and (viii) 'a mere tasting, a small quantity, a mouthful'. In Late Modern English one more sense was added, which reintroduced (partially) the association with SMELL, i.e., (ix) 'a touch or suggestion of sth having a characteristic odour or taste'.

Even though the dictionary sources indicate that *smæc* was used already in the Old English period with reference to the semantic fields of both TASTE and SMELL, *the Helsinki Corpus* shows no occurrence of the noun, whilst *the Toronto Corpus* contains only three instances: two with reference to TASTE (1) and one to SMELL (2):

(1)   In goman, þær mon þone **smæc** todæleþ
(2)   Swete **smæc** (= Lat. dulcis odor)

(TC: Latin-Old English glossaries)

In Middle English, the noun was much more frequent. It was represented by two forms: *smack* which developed from the OE *smæc* and *smatch*[2], an alternation of the Old English form which developed under the influence of the Old English verb *smeccan* 'to have a (specified) flavour or taste' (*OED*).

The noun was found 56 times in the Middle English corpora (31 occurrences of *smack* and 25 of the affricated form). It should be noticed that *smack* was found

---

2   The *MED* treats both as different spellings of the same word, whilst *the OED* treats them as separate lexemes, suggesting that *smatch* was used exclusively with reference to TASTE. Due to the overlapping of various spellings of both forms, the differentiation between the two was extremely difficult, thus, we have decided to follow the approach presented in the *MED*.

exclusively with reference to TASTE (3), whilst *smatch* was recorded with reference to both senses: SMELL, e.g., (4) and TASTE, e.g., (5), which is in exact opposition to the information found in *the OED*.

(3) ase þet zalt yefþ **smac** to þe mete

(IC: Ayenbite of inwyt)

(4) ... & of his nease-þurles þreste smorðrinde smoke, **smecche** forcuðest;

(IC: Seinte Marherete)

(5) þet is þe fehereste deal. bitweonen muðes **smech**. & neases smeal.

(IC: Ancrene riwle)

Additionally, the gerundive form *smatching*, used in a nominal context, was found 15 times, denoting 'the sense of taste', e.g., (6) – (7). What is interesting is that not a single record of *smatch* was found with such a meaning, which suggests that *smatching* took over this particular sense of the noun. This did not apply to the non-affricated form, since *smack* did occur with the meaning 'the sense of taste', e.g., (8).

(6) Sihðe & herunge, **smechunge** & smellunge, & euch limes felunge;

(IC: Hali meidenhad)

(7) nis nout spellunge þe muðes wit ase **smecchunge**. Þauh heo beon beoðe ine muðe

(IC: Ancrene riwle)

(8) GIET me wreið min herte of ða fif wittes ðe god me (be)tahte to lokin of mine wrecche lichame, þat is, visus, auditus, gustus, odoratus, et tactus, þat is, ʒesihthe, ʒeherhþe, **smac**, and smell, and tactþe.

(IC: Vices and virtues)

Neither *smack* nor *smatch* were found in the Early Modern English corpora. According to *the EDD*, they became dialectal. The former was recorded in Scotland and Lakeland, meaning 'taste' (9),

(9) Ah've a queer **smach** i' mi mooth

(EDD: s.v. smack sb[1])

whilst the latter, meaning 'a flavour, taste' (10), became limited to the local dialects of North Country, Durham, Cumberland, Yorkshire, Lancashire, Chesire, Derby, Leicester, Warwick, Worcester, Oxford, Hampshire and Dorset (see Fig. 1). It should be mentioned that *smatch* occurred also figuratively, meaning 'taint' (11).

(10) Whey burnt in boiling has a **smatch**.
(11) A **smatch** of London in their talk.

(EDD: s.v. smatch)

The reference specifically to 'the sense of taste' has not been recorded in *the EDD*.

Fig. 1. Early Modern English occurrences of *smatch* (*EDD*).

The dominance of the reference to TASTE is very well visible in the history of the noun. The evidence from the Old English period is too scarce to draw any conclusions (only three cases were found). However, in the Middle English corpora the number of occurrences of various forms of *smack* with reference to TASTE outnumbers those referring to SMELL (see Fig. 2). Thus, the disappearance of the latter from the Early Modern English has been of no surprise.

	smack		*smatch*		*smatching*	
	TASTE	SMELL	TASTE	SMELL	TASTE	SMELL
Old English	2	1	–	–	–	–
Middle English	31	–	21	4	15	–

Fig. 2. Number of occurrences of various forms of *smack* with reference to the semantic fields of TASTE and SMELL.

2.2 OE/ME *swæc*

OE *swæc* shared its referential meaning between the semantic fields of TASTE and SMELL. It was recorded in *the Anglo-Saxon Dictionary* with the senses (i) 'a taste, flavour, savour', (ii) 'the sense of taste', (iii) 'odour, smell, scent' and (iv) 'the sense of smell'. Following *the MED*, it entered the Middle English period with senses (i) and (iii), thus, it continued to apply to both semantic fields, however, lost its reference to the particular senses.

The Toronto Corpus records 78 occurrences of the lexeme. Over half of them refer to TASTE, e.g., (12) – (14). The rest but three were applied to SMELL, e.g., (15) – (17). Two of the occurrences were found impossible to classify, whilst one record denotes 'speech' (18), even though none of the dictionaries list such a sense. The ratio of the various senses of *swæc* are shown in Fig. 3 below.

(12) þæt ys we scyolon ure yfelnysse behreowsian mid urum fif andgytum þæt synt: gesyhð and hlyst and **swæc** and stenc and hrepung;

(TC: Purification)

(13) þa fif getyma getacniað þa fif andgitu ures lichaman. þæt sind Gesihð. Hlyst. **Swæcc**. Stenc. Hrepung;

(TC: Third Sunday after pentecost)

(14) þæt is swutellice to secgenne þæt se mete awende, on þæs mannes muðe þe þone mete æt, to þæs metes **swæcce** þe him sylfum gelicode, swa hu swa he wolde habban to gereorde.

(TC: De populo Israhel)

(15) me eadmodne þeow ðinne syle me heortan seo þe ondræde sefan se þe ongyte eagan þa þe geseon earan þa þe gehyran nosa þa **swæcc** þinne underfon.

(TC: Prayers)

(16) L olfactum = stenc, **swæc**.

(TC: Latin-Old English glossaries)

(17) þonne he mid winde ahafen bið, swa hwær swa hy beoð hy þone **swæc** gestincað, hy sculon sweltan.

(TC: Pseudo-Apuleius: Herbarium)

(18) Na synd **swæca** na word þara na synd stefne heora. = L Non sunt **loquele** neque sermons quorum non audiantur uoces eorum.

(TC: Psalms)

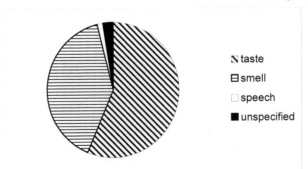

Fig. 3. The ratio of the Old English senses of *swæc*, as recorded in *the Toronto Corpus*.

When used to denote one of the senses (either 'the sense of smell' or 'the sense of taste'), the meaning of the noun could be verified due to the presence of the unambiguous lexemes in the close neighbourhood of *swæc*, e.g., in (19) *swæc* refers to 'the sense of taste', since 'the sense of smell' is represented by the unequivocal *stynce*, whilst in (20) – (21) *swæc* stands for 'the sense of smell' since 'the sense of taste' is represented by the monoreferential *byrgincge* 'taste'. However, in a number of cases, when the neighbourhood of the noun is not helpful, the categorisation of the noun becomes more complicated and sometimes even impossible, thus a few records were not classified (see Fig. 3).

(19) on gesihðe on leahtre, on gehernesse on **swæcce**, on **stynce** on hrepunge, on leasre
      gewitnysse, on gytsunge on manslihte

                                        (*TC: Forms of confession and absolution*)

(20) on gesihðe on hlyste on **byrgincge** on **swæcce** æthrine þu soðlice mildheorta god
      to gewyrcenne me sawle minre hæle lima syndrige menniscum brycum gemæte þu
      sealdest

                                                      (*TC: Prayers*)

(21) dracontea on stanigum lande wyxð, heo ys hnesce on æthrine weredre on **byrincge**
      on **swæce** swylce grene cystel, se wyrtruma neoðeweard swylce dracan heafod
                                        (*TC*: Pseudo-Apuleius*: Herbarium*)

Although, *the MED* lists *swæc* with the senses 'an odour, aroma' and 'taste, flavour', the corpora data show only a single record of the noun, with reference to SMELL, see (22). Such limitation in use shows the process of disappearance of the noun, which led to its obsolescence.

(22) He lædde me þagyt furðer, & ic geseh þær ætforen us mycele mare liht, & ic þære
      wynsume stæme ormætes dreames geherde, & wunderlices bræðes **swæc** of þære
      stowe ut fleow.
                                        (*IC: Early English homilies from the 12th c.*)

2.3 OE *hunigsmæc* and OE *sealt*

The two nouns, even though listed as synonyms of *taste* in its general sense, both in the Old English corpora as well as in *the Anglo-Saxon Dictionary*, were used with a specific meaning, referring to a particular quality of taste. Thus, they will not be discussed in the present paper.

2.4 *byrg*-derivatives

The derivatives of *byrg* were found only in the Old English corpora (25 records). Their reference was limited to the semantic field of TASTE, both in its general meaning and denoting 'the sense of taste'. Majority of the former were applied to negative tastes, e.g., poisonous (23) or bitter (24) – (25). The latter meaning has been exemplified in (26) – (27).

(23) Wið attres **onbyrgingce** genim þas (ilcan) wyrte, cnuca on ecede, syle drincan.
(*TC*: Pseudo-Apuleius: *Herbarium*)

(24) Heo bið hnesce on æthrine bittere on **byrgingce**.
(*TC*: Pseudo-Apuleius: *Herbarium*)

(25) þeos wyrt byþ cenned on morum, heo hafaþ leaf sinewealte, ða bittere on **byrgincge**, heo hafaþ feowerecgedne stelan fealuwe blostman.
(*TC*: Pseudo-Apuleius: *Herbarium*)

(26) swa hwilce þing on gesyhþe on hlyste on **onbyrginge** on steame oþþe on æthrine gemeleaslice ongylte mid manifealdum unalyfedum wyrcende geþwærigende = L. et quaecumque in visu auditu **gustu** odoratu vel tactu neglegenter commisi multiplicibus inlicitis operando vel consentiendo
(*TC*: *Prayers*)

(27) **anbyrignys** = L. Gustus
(*TC*: *Latin-Old English glossaries*)

Neither the analyzed dictionaries nor textual corpora show any record of the *byrg-*derivatives in the Middle English period.

2.5 ME *savour*; LME *sapor*

Savour was borrowed into English in the 13th c. from OF *savur, savour*, which in turn was borrowed from Latin *saporem* 'taste'. The latter also served as a source of borrowing for English *sapour*, which when introduced in the 15th c. duplicated *savour* agreeing both in its form and (partially) in meaning.

Savour entered English with the senses (i) 'a taste or flavour' and (ii) 'relish or taste for sth; delight, satisfaction' (*MED*). The meaning extended a century later, when sense (iii) 'a smell, perfume, aroma' was added (now poetic or archaic). In the 15th c. further senses were added: (iv) 'the sense or faculty of taste' and (v) 'the faculty or sense of smell; the action of smelling'.

Apart from the senses referring to the senses of smell and taste, *savour* occurred meaning 'a characteristic, tendency, inherent nature' and 'pleasure, delight', however, due to the great number of occurrences of the noun, we will concentrate on the records connected to the topic of the present paper.

The number of occurrences with reference to each of the semantic fields was similar. The Middle English corpora show that in 32% of cases, *savour* points to the semantic field TASTE, while 44% of records – to SMELL. 24.% of occurrences carried non-sensual meaning. The ratio of the records of *savour* with particular senses is shown in Fig. 4. In both semantic fields, the noun was used with reference to pleasant and offensive smells or tastes, respectively, see (28) – (31), as well as with a general reference. No record was found with sense (v) 'the sense of smell', whilst (iv) 'the sense of taste' was represented by less than 2% of the examples referring to TASTE, e.g., (32).

(28) ... thereto he smelleth so sweet, that the **savour** of him boteth all sickness; and for his beauty and sweet smelling all other beasts follow him, for by his sweet **savour** they ben healed of all sickness.

(IC: Caxton's translation of *The history of Reynard the Fox)*

(29) By þin nose, not bot eiþer stynche or **sauour**. & by þi taast, not bot eiþer soure or swete, salt or fresche, bittyr or likyng.

(IC: Cloud of unknowing and the Book of privy counselling)

(30) Also þis herbe is swet of **sauour**. þe vertu of þis herbe.

(IC: Agnus Castus: *A Middle English herbal)*

(31) þan frete thi teeth with barke or with sum thing that is of drie and hoot complexioun and of bittir **savoure**, for þat makith the teeth clene, and distroyeth the yville savoure of the mouthe, and also it makith the voyce clere, and yevith appetite to mete;

(IC: Three prose versions of the Secreta Secretorum)

(32) And forther-over, they shul have defaute of alle manere delyces; for certes, delyces been after the appetytes of the fyve wittes, as sighte, heringe, smellinge, **savoringe**, and touchinge.

(IC: The Parson's tale)

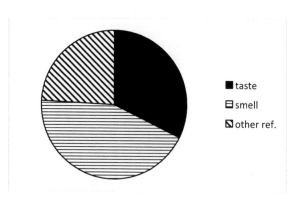

Fig. 4. The ratio of the Middle English senses of *savour*.

In a number of examples, *savour* occurred together with its synonym(s), see (33) - (34).

(33) This wyn shal be wel lykyng in **sauour, odour**, or **smellyng**.
(*IC: A Middle English translation of Macer Floridus de Viribus herbarum*)

(34) þis is þat precious gostly mete & speciale mynde of oure lorde Jesu, in þe whiche is hade alle gostly likyng, & þe **sauour & taste** of alle swetnes.
(*IC: Mirror of the blessed life of Jesus Christ*)

The use of synonyms in pairs or even in series might have been caused by the writer's strive to be exact. If, on the one hand, we assume that the binominals were not fully synonymous, the use of doublets or even triplets becomes justified, as they might have complemented one another. Moreover, taking into consideration the foreign origin of some of the components making up the repetition series, the assumption that some of the items might have been obscure to the reader also explains the repetition. However, on the other hand, taking into account the frequency of occurrence of the discussed nouns, the latter explanation seems dubious. Thus, the most convincing reason for the use of synonyms seems to be the difference in meaning, even though the dictionary sources do not confirm it, we have to remember that full synonymy is hardly possible. The nouns most probably differed in the shades of meaning, thus writers juxtaposed them. The historical character of the material imposes limitations on our research, thus the degree of synonymy of the words may not be possible to verify.

According to the *MED*, at the end of the 14th c., a related form, i.e., *sapor* entered English. It was borrowed from Latin, in which it referred exclusively to the semantic field TASTE. The analysed corpora enumerate the noun only in Latin fragments: twelve times in Old English and only twice in the Middle English corpora. The former provided translation, in which *swæc* was the usual Old English equivalent, see (35), with the exception of one occurrence where *sapor* was explained by OE *stenc*[3]. In Middle English *sapor* occurred in the form of quotation, without providing a translation, which suggests that the reader was expected to understand the Latin fragment, see (36).

(35) Fundens aroma cortice vincens **saporem** nectaris foecunda fructu fertili portans triumphum nobilem
= ageotende wyrtbræð of rinde ofer swiþende **swæce** hunigteare ecne on wæstme wæstmbærum berende sige æþelne.
(*TC: Hymns*)

(36) Erest it beð ouelete and win. and þureh þe holi word þe ure helende him self seide mid his holi muð and efter him prest hem seið ate swimesse turneð þe bred to fleis and þe win to blod. Set in carne remanet forma color et **sapor**. ac on þe holi fleis bileueð þe shap and hiu. and smul of ouelete on þe holi blod hew & smul of win.
(*IC: OE Homilies of the 12th c.*)

---

3   Such a translation of *sapor* suggests a misinterpretation of the Latin noun – OE *stenc* referred exclusively to the semantic field SMELL, cf. Bator (2009: 74-76).

2.6 ME *taste*

In the 14th c. the noun *taste* was borrowed from French *tast* 'touching, touch'. When introduced into English, it was recorded with the following senses (i) 'taste as an inherent property of matter; flavour', (ii) 'the sense of taste'; and (iii) 'the sense of touch, the ability to feel or perceive'. At the beginning, the noun shared its referential field between the semantic fields of TASTE and TOUCH. A century after its introduction, the meaning extended to (iv) 'the sense of smell' and (v) 'smell, odour, scent', dividing the referential field of *taste* to a still another semantic field and still another sense, i.e., SMELL.

A great majority of records of *taste* found in the Middle English corpora show reference to the semantic field TASTE (75%), e.g., (37) – (38).

(37) … swete smelles in þeire noses, wonderful **taastes** in þeire mowþes, & many queynte hetes & brennynges in þeire bodily brestes or in þeire bowelles, in þeire backes & in þeire reynes, & in þeire pryue membres.

(IC: Cloud of unknowing and the Book of privy counselling)

(38) By þin nose, not bot eiþer stynche or sauour. & by þi **taast**, not bot eiþer soure or swete, salt or fresche, bittyr or likyng.

(IC: Cloud of unknowing and the Book of privy counselling)

Only 6% of records were used to denote 'smell', e.g., (39). And single occurrences of *taste* indicate the original meaning of the noun, i.e., 'touch' (only 1.5%), see (40).

(39) hit happed soo that they were thursty and they sawe a lytyl flacked of gold stande by them and hit semed by the coloure and the **taste** that it was noble wyn Thenne sire Trystram toke the flacket in his hand and sayd Madame Isoud here is the best drynke that euer ye drank that dame Bragwayne youre mayden and Gouernayle my seruaunt haue kepte for them self

(IC: Malory: Le morte d'Arthur)

(40) The **taste** is a commyn witte, Spraden throgh the body, but hit Shewyth hym most by he handys than any othyr lym of the body; by that witte we knowen hote, colde, dry, moyste, and othyr Suche thynges.

(IC: Three prose versions of Secreta secretorum)

The original denotation of *taste* points to only one sense, i.e., TOUCH. When borrowed into English the noun's meaning referred also to another sense, very close semantically, i.e., TASTE. The scarce number of examples of *taste* meaning 'touch' as well as the growing frequency of the latter sense, may account for the obsolescence of the original meaning of the noun. The later extension of the reference to yet another sense (SMELL) may be justified by the contiguity of the two senses (TASTE and SMELL). Over 70% of what we perceive as taste comes from our sense of smell. Thus, the linguistic connection between the two senses may be explained by the natural contiguity of the two. Fig. 5 presents the ratio of meanings with which *taste* occurred throughout the Middle English period, as recorded in the analysed Middle English corpora.

The transfer of reference of *taste* from touch to taste and then to smell agrees with Williams' (1976) schedule of transfer of sensory meaning. According to Williams, there is a strict direction in which sensory words may change denotation. Thus, a touch-word may transfer to taste, colour or sound. A taste-word, in turn, may transfer to smell or sound. Smell-words are not supposed to shift to other senses. The direction of the shift of meanings of *taste* also agrees with Aristotle's order of senses: touch – taste – smell – hearing – sight, where touch is the primary sense, whilst sight the most advanced one. Moreover, according to Aristotle, taste is a type of touch, which would account for the extension of the original reference of the borrowing.

Similarly to *savour*, *taste* was used to compose repetitive pairs, e.g., (41). However, the process was not as frequent as in the case of *savour*. This may be accounted for by the fact that the number of records of *savour* was almost five times bigger than those of *taste*.

(41) Teres of penaunce be wyne of angels, for in hem is odoure of lyfe, sauour of grace, taste of indulgence.

(IC: Speculum Christiani)

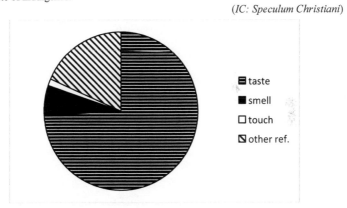

Fig. 5. The ratio of the Middle English senses of *taste*.

2.7 ME minor nouns

Apart from the nouns discussed so far, there were a number of lexical items which either referred to TASTE marginally, e.g., *tang, tarage* and *sentiment*, or were used with extremely low frequency or for a short period, e.g., *gust* and *relese (relish)*.

2.7.1 ME *relese (relish)*

ME *relese* was probably derived from AN or MF *reles, relais* 'residue'. Its first record comes from the 14th c. when it was used with the following senses: (i) 'impression, effect, influence' – this sense probably developed from the French meaning; (ii) 'taste, relish', and (iii) 'odour, scent'. The *MED* adds (iv) 'beauty'. The form *relese* was in use until the beginning of the 17th c., however, from the 16th c. an assimilated form *relish* surfaced in English[4]. The latter was recorded with numerous senses, all of which referred to the semantic field TASTE: (a) 'a taste or flavour; the distinctive taste of sth' (obs.), (b) 'enjoyment of the taste or flavour of sth', (c) 'an individual taste or liking' (obs.), (d) 'the sense of taste' (obs.), and in the 18th c. the meaning (e) 'sth of savoury or piquant taste' was added.

The sensory denotation of *relese* has been found neither in the Middle English nor the Early Modern English corpora. The later form, *relish*, was found only twice in *the Lampeter Corpus* (EModE), both records with sense (b). Such a small number of occurrences proves the infrequency of the noun, which led to the displacement of *relese* and obsolescence of three of the five senses of the noun.

2.7.2 ME *gust*

Gust, of Latin origin, entered English in the 15th c. In the Middle English period *gust* denoted (i) 'the sense or faculty of taste'. In Early Modern English its meaning extended to: (ii) 'an act of tasting or of satisfying the appetite', (iii) 'individual taste, liking' (obs.), (iv) 'aesthetic or artistic taste, sense or perception' (obs.), (v) 'savour or flavour of food', and (vi) 'a taste, an experience of sth' (obs.).

Only a single occurrence of *gust* was found (42):

(42) The Answer I make, to those that will say, Every Body knew this Story before, is, That tho' I pretend to Write Novel's, I don't Novelties, but to dress up something that for one Meal may be Pleasing, and of grateful **Gust**; and perhaps some Observation may be made from this Story worthy Self-Application: But tho' the Reader do not, I will, to continue the Method I first Design'd.
                          (*LC: Labour in vain: or, What signifies little or nothing*)

2.7.3 ME *tang*

The primary meaning of ME *tang* was 'a projecting pointed part or instrument'. It joined the semantic field TASTE in the 15th c., when the sense 'a penetrating taste or flavour' was added. This sense survived in the Early Modern English dialects. The *EDD* records *tang* meaning 'a strong or peculiar taste or flavour, esp. an

---

4   An assimilation of the ending to *-ish* suffix took place.

unpleasant one' in the dialects of Scotland, Lancashire, Lincoln, Hereford, East Anglia, Suffolk, Kent, Isle of Wight, Devon, and Cornwall.

2.7.4 ME *tarage, tallage*

Throughout the 15th c., *tarage* was in use, denoting 'taste, flavour' as well as 'the quality, character, esp. as derived or communicated'. In the late 15th c. its doublet, i.e., *tallage* appeared with the meaning (i) 'taste, savour' and (ii) 'the sense of taste'. Both forms became obsolete, the former in the late 15th c., the latter in the 17th c. Neither has been found in any of the analysed corpora.

2.7.5 ME *sentiment*

Sentiment was borrowed from OF *sentiment* in the 14th c. and referred to various kinds of feelings. *The OED* records a single occurrence of the noun with the sense 'flavour' (43).

> (43) And other Trees there ben also, that beren wyn of noble **sentement**.
> (*OED: s.v. sentiment* [*Mandeville's travels*])

3. Conclusion

As has been demonstrated above, the semantic field TASTE was highly restructured in the Middle English period. Only one of the Old English lexemes has survived in the language, however, not without a serious limitation in usage. Such a situation was caused by the influence of more prestigious borrowings from French.

In the Middle English period a number of new words were introduced, the most important ones being *savour* and *taste*. Both of them shared their referential field between the senses of TASTE and SMELL, which might have been caused by the natural contiguity and mutual influence of both senses on each other. *Savour*, which in Middle English was applied slightly more frequently to the sense of smell than taste (see Fig. 4), retained its reference to both senses. *Taste* narrowed its meaning by losing a number of senses and its reference to the sense of taste became the dominant one, which contributed to the fact that the noun became the primary lexical item within the words belonging to the semantic field TASTE. All the other nouns constituting the semantic field in the Middle English period, either lost their reference to TASTE or became limited in usage, and thus do not play any important role within the field.

References

Bator, Magdalena
   2009   "Sense and inventory changes in the semantic field 'smell' in the history
           of English", *Inozemna Philologia* 121: 72-79.
Bosworth, Joseph – T. Northcote Toller (eds.)
   1972-2002 *An Anglo-Saxon Dictionary*. Oxford: Oxford University Press.
Kay, Christian – Jane Roberts – Michael Samuels – Irene Wotherspoon (eds.)
   2009   *Historical thesaurus of English*. Oxford: Oxford University Press.
Markus, Manfred (et al.) (eds.)
   2009   *The Innsbruck corpus of Middle English prose.* (on CD-ROM, version
           2.3).
Middle English Dictionary online, available at: http://quod.lib.umich.edu/m/med/
Oxford English Dictionary online, available at: www.oed.com
Rissanen, Matti (et al.) (eds.)
   1991   *The Helsinki Corpus of English texts: Diachronic and dialectal.* Helsinki:
           The University of Helsinki.
Schmied, Josef – Claudia Claridge – Rainer Siemund (eds.)
   1999   *The Lampeter Corpus of Early Modern English tracts,* available at:
           http://www.ota.ox.ac.uk/headers/2400.xml
Thesaurus of Old English online, available at: http://libra.englang.arts.gla.ac.uk
           /oethesaurus/menutoe.html
Williams, Joseph M.
   1976   "Synaesthetic adjectives: A possible law of semantic change", *Language*
           52.2: 461-478.
Wright, Joseph (ed.)
   1898-1905 *The English dialect dictionary*. Oxford: Oxford University Press.

Medieval English Mirror

Edited by Marcin Krygier and Liliana Sikorska

Vol. 1 Marcin Krygier / Liliana Sikorska (eds.): For the Loue of Inglis Lede. 2004.

Vol. 2 Marcin Krygier / Liliana Sikorska (eds.): Naked Wordes in Englissh. 2005.

Vol. 3 Marcin Krygier / Liliana Sikorska (eds.): To Make his Englissh Sweete upon his Tonge. 2007.

Vol. 4 Marcin Krygier / Liliana Sikorska (eds.): The Propur Langage of Englische Men. Assistants to the editors: Ewa Ciszek and Łukasz Hudomięt. 2008.

Vol. 5 Marcin Krygier / Liliana Sikorska (eds.): Þe Laurer of Oure Englische Tonge. Assistants to the editors: Ewa Ciszek and Łukasz Hudomięt. 2009.

Vol. 6 Marcin Krygier / Liliana Sikorska (eds.): Þe comoun peplis language. Assistants to the editors: Ewa Ciszek and Katarzyna Bronk. 2010.

Vol. 7 Liliana Sikorska (ed.): Thise Stories Beren Witnesse. The Landscape of the Afterlife in Medieval and Post-Medieval Imagination. Assistant to the editor: Katarzyna Bronk. 2010.

Vol. 8 Marcin Krygier (ed.): Of fair speche, and of fair answere. Assistant to the editor: Ewa Ciszek. 2013.

www.peterlang.de